James McNair's
BREAKFAST

Revised Edition

Inside Photography by Patricia Brabant
Cover Photography by James McNair

CHRONICLE BOOKS

SAN FRANCISCO

Printed in Hong Kong.

*Library of Congress
Cataloging-in-Publication Data:*

McNair, James K.
    James McNair's breakfast/inside photography by
Patricia Brabant; cover photography by James McNair.
        p. cm.
    Includes index.
    ISBN 0-8118-2061-0 (pb)
    1. Breakfasts. 2. Brunches. I. Title.
TX733.M479 1998   97-39664
641.5'2–dc21   CIP

Distributed in Canada by
Raincoast Books
8680 Cambie Street
Vancouver, British Columbia V6P 6M9

10 9 8 7 6 5 4 3 2 1

Chronicle Books
85 Second Street
San Francisco, CA 94105

Web Site: www.chronbooks.com

For the special people with whom I've enjoyed countless breakfasts:

James and Lucille McNair, my parents, and Martha McNair, my sister, with memories of the braised quail breakfasts of Christmases past;

Lenny Meyer, my companion of years gone by, who taught me to enjoy coffee and eggs and introduced me to bagels, smoked salmon, and Zabar's Russian coffee cake;

Lin Cotton, my late partner, with whom I originally planned this book over morning coffee and waffles made from his mom's butter-rich recipe;

and Andrew Moore, my partner, also known as Mr. Sunshine, who thrives on the simple pleasures of steaming hot oatmeal and fresh fruit.

In the original edition of this book, I offered a hearty welcome to the world to Devereux McNair, my first nephew, whose birth was announced to me during the photography session for grillades and grits, a treat that my brother-in-law, John Richardson, prepares for our holiday brunches. Devereux has since been joined by a brother, Ryan Richardson, who prefers ice cream for breakfast.

Editorial and photographic production by James McNair and Andrew Moore, The Rockpile Press, San Francisco and Lake Tahoe, California

**Art direction, photographic and food styling, and book design by James McNair
Studio kitchen assistance by Gail High
Photographic assistance to Patricia Brabant by Louis Block**

Typography and mechanical production by Cleve Gallat

Contents

INTRODUCTION

Nutritionists advocate breakfast as the most important meal of the day. It also happens to be my favorite meal. Such was not always the case, however.

Like too many youngsters, I hated breakfast and skipped it whenever my mother allowed. Back then I'd much rather sleep late than eat, so I usually wolfed down a piece of toast or a bowl of cold cereal before making the two-block dash to school. I detested eggs in any form—probably because they were always overcooked for my taste, I later discovered. My morning meal habits only got worse during college and graduate school, where I usually downed a Coke and a package of cupcakes or doughnuts en route to class across campus. I'll never know how much more I might have gotten out of school if I'd taken time for a good breakfast.

During those formative years, there were occasional exceptions to my anti-breakfast attitude. For as long as I can remember, the traditional Christmas morning feast in our home centered around quail that my daddy killed, my mother braised, and my sister and I ate with gusto. And somehow I always managed to have plenty of time and a hearty appetite for breakfast whenever my mother cooked pancakes or waffles.

Likewise, I enjoyed breakfast whenever we went to Mississippi to visit Mamaw and Papaw Keith, Uncle Sanford, Aunt Doris, and Cousin Sandra Kay. Whether breakfast was served in their roomy kitchen by the wood cookstove in the old plantation house out from Pickins, or later in their gentrified neighborhood of Jackson, I found the thick slices of smoked ham, piping-hot white biscuits, homemade jelly, sliced Cheddar cheese, and occasional garden-ripe tomatoes worth getting up early for.

When I moved on my own to New Orleans, I discovered the pleasures of breakfasting Creole style—at any hour of the day—on hot *beignets* dusted with powdered sugar, grillades and grits, or fried rice *calas*. Recipes for all those happily remembered tastes are included in this book.

A few years later, in New York City, my taste for breakfast foods expanded greatly. My friend Lenny Meyer slowly converted me to coffee and eggs and introduced me to the pleasures of bagels, smoked salmon and whitefish, and Zabar's Russian coffee cake. While shopping in the dawning hours of the morning for flowers and plants for a retail boutique, my business partners Richard Champion and Bob Springman and I planned the daily schedule over stacks of pancakes or delectable French toast in a tiny Greek coffee shop tucked into the bustling flower market. And for several years I frequently enjoyed my own version of *Breakfast at Tiffany's*, munching on take-out deli corn muffins and sipping freshly squeezed orange juice while arranging flowers for the store's table settings.

The past two decades-plus of living in California have seen another expansion of my breakfast repertoire. Whether in retreat during my writing periods or entertaining a houseful of friends, I enjoy getting up and filling the air with the aromas of strong coffee, freshly cut fruits, and grain-rich muffins, oven-puffed pancakes, or crunchy corn pancakes studded with plump blueberries.

Most of us use up more energy during the morning hours and therefore need the long-lasting fuel provided by a well-balanced meal. The heaviest concentration of recipes in this book lies in the dishes made from grains, rich in the carbohydrates that leave us feeling satisfied. I've tried to favor *complex* carbohydrates (starches), found in whole grains, which fuel our bodies with energy and can be burned off during an active day. With the exception of the natural sugar found in fruits, we all need to downplay the *simple* carbohydrates (the sugars). This doesn't mean giving up maple syrup on pancakes, just being judicious.

The ideal breakfast also includes adequate protein. In addition to meats, or alternatively, this can come from cheese, yogurt, eggs, nut butters, and whole grains combined with legumes, seeds, or nuts.

Much has been said about the need for fiber at breakfast. A diet rich in whole grains and whole fruits is a much tastier way of getting that fiber than is ruining a good glass of juice by stirring bran or other fiber products into it.

If you need or wish to cut down on fats at breakfast, choose lean cuts of meat instead of bacon or sausage (enjoy these old favorites only on special occasions); steam, poach, or bake meats instead of frying; use nonstick cookware that requires little or no fat; coat pans with vegetable-oil spray instead of using butter or oil; use skimmed or low-fat dairy products; substitute yogurt for sour cream; use butter in moderation or blend it with part safflower or other high-polyunsaturated margarine, or choose a reduced-fat brand of spread (avoid spreads that use unhealthy hydrogenated oils).

Most of the recipes in this collection emphasize good nutrition. There are, however, scattered recipes for dishes rich in fats and sweeteners for those special occasions when indulgence seems justified. I certainly don't advocate eating this way day after day, but we can enjoy those dishes from time to time as long as our standard breakfasts emphasize foods that are fairly low in fat, adequate in protein, and high in complex carbohydrates. The key to good nutrition at any time of the day is a well-balanced diet that includes a wide variety of foods—not the same English muffin and fried egg or bowl of granola day after day.

But I find breakfast to be much more than just the main energizing meal of the day. Through the years the morning meal has provided me with some of life's most pleasurable moments. Whether it's Bellinis and puffed oven-baked pancakes at a table set with crisp linens, beautiful dishes, and fresh flowers for a cheerful celebration with friends, or a solitary caffèlatte and a fresh apple muffin in a peaceful nook, a relaxed breakfast sets the tone for a happy and productive day.

May this book add pleasure to your mornings.

BEVERAGES & FRUITS

Coffee

Your morning cup will be only as good as the coffee beans you buy and the equipment you choose for brewing. Coffee flavor and strength, however, is a matter of taste. Beans from the various coffee-growing regions of the world produce different flavors and the type of roasting determines the darkness and intensity of flavor; French or Italian roasts are the most intense. Whether regular or decaffeinated, and whatever the bean or the roast, be sure the coffee is absolutely fresh by buying from a reliable dealer. For maximum flavor, buy whole beans, store only as much as you can use in a few days' time in a tightly closed container in a cool place, and grind only as much as you need for each pot; consult the coffee equipment manufacturer's directions for the correct grind. Freeze extra beans in an airtight container.

As a general rule, use 1 standard coffee scoop (2 level tablespoons) of freshly ground regular or decaffeinated coffee to each ¾ cup of water. Adjust this measurement to your taste.

I prefer making coffee in one of two ways. If the brew will be used immediately, I often use a plunger system pot. Place the coffee grounds in the bottom of the clear glass beaker fitted inside a metal or plastic frame. Add water that's been brought just to a boil and let it stand for about 5 minutes before plunging down the tightly fitting mesh filter, which traps the grounds in the bottom of the pot.

When planning to sip longer, I prefer to drip the coffee through a gold-mesh or paper filter into an insulated pot that will keep the drink hot for several hours without further heating, which destroys the flavor. These days I favor an electronic maker that drips directly into a thermal pot, but it may be done manually. Place the filter in the plastic cone that fits on top of the pot, add the freshly ground coffee, pour water that's been brought just to a boil over the grounds, remove the cone after the coffee has dripped, and screw on the tightly fitting cap.

If you choose to use an electric coffee maker that drips the brew into a glass pot on a heating element, be sure to make only enough to be used within a few minutes. Otherwise the coffee will burn from sitting on the heating element. Or for longer keeping, immediately pour the coffee into a heated insulated pot. Avoid percolators or other pots that use too high a heat and boil—thus ruin—good coffee.

No matter what type of coffee maker you choose, be sure it is immaculately clean before brewing. Coffee leaves an oily film inside the pot that can taint the flavor of fresh coffee.

Milk added to coffee helps neutralize the acid in the brew and provides some nutrition. I always heat low-fat milk in a saucepan or in a pitcher in the microwave, both to enhance the milk's flavor and to avoid cooling the coffee. If you enjoy a richer milk, select whole milk, half and half, or cream; just leave that nondairy stuff on the shelf. Although I feel that coffee tastes best without any sweetener, add sugar or a substitute to taste.

ESPRESSO is made from dark, double-roasted beans that are ground to a fine powder. Authentic espresso can be made only in an electric or stove-top espresso maker where water is forced by high pressure through the coffee. Follow the espresso maker manufacturer's instructions. Add a twist of lemon peel if desired.

CAPPUCCINO is espresso coffee topped with the thick foam that results from steaming milk in a machine that has a spigot for steaming. Make espresso in a large cup, follow the manufacturer's instructions for steaming the milk, spoon the resulting foam onto the top of the coffee, and sprinkle with cinnamon or powdered sweet chocolate if desired.

CAFFÈ LATTE combines equal portions of espresso with steamed milk, topped off with the foam from steaming. Pour espresso into a mug or heat-resistant glass, pour in the steamed milk, sprinkle with ground cinnamon or sweetened grated chocolate if desired.

CAFÉ AU LAIT combines strong dark-roast coffee with milk that's heated to just under the boiling point. Make a pot of coffee, heat milk in a microwave or in a saucepan, and pour the two into a cup or mug to taste, usually in equal portions.

Don't forget the possibility of serving iced coffee on hot mornings. Refrigerate a pot of freshly made coffee in an airtight container overnight for serving at breakfast. Serve over ice with cold milk and sweetener as desired.

Black Tea

Although tea bags are quick and easy, a perfect pot of tea starts with good-quality loose tea. While you are bringing a kettle of freshly drawn cold water just to a boil, warm a clean nonmetal teapot with hot water, then drain. Place 1 teaspoon of tea leaves in the pot for each cup of water you will add, plus a traditional extra one "for the pot." Pour the boiling water over the tea leaves and steep for 3 to 5 minutes; cover the pot with a quilted or insulated tea cozy to keep the tea hot. Fill a second teapot with boiling water for adjusting the strength of the brew in the cup. Stir the tea once to distribute the flavor and pour through a strainer into teacups or glasses. Add a sweetener, milk, or lemon if you wish.

To prepare hot-weather iced tea, pour boiling water over the tea leaves and steep until very strong, about 15 minutes. Pour into a pitcher and add cold water to the desired strength. Serve over ice with fresh mint, lemon or orange slices or juice, and a sweetener if desired.

VARIATIONS: Mix into any dry tea leaves some dried or fresh herb leaves, pesticide-free rose or other fragrant flower petals, bits of lemon or orange peel, pieces of vanilla bean, or whole spices such as cloves or pieces of cinnamon stick. Blend well and store in an airtight container.

Herbal Tea

Keep in mind that herbal beverages are made from the same plant parts as many medicines; in some people they can cause as many problems as the caffeine of coffee or black tea may cause, so use judiciously.

Drinks made from the leaves of one kind of herb or a mixture of herbs are made by *infusion*, or steeping in hot water. Bring freshly drawn cold water to a boil. Meanwhile, warm a clean nonmetal teapot with hot water, then drain. For each cup of water, place 2 to 3 teaspoons fresh herb leaves, or 1 to 2 teaspoons dried herb leaves, in the pot. Cover with the boiling water and steep from 5 to 10 minutes, covering the pot with a tea cozy to keep the brew warm. Strain into cups and add sweeteners or lemon if you wish.

Drinks made from seeds, roots, or bark are made by *decoction*, or boiling in water, to bring out the flavor. Place the plant part in a pot of water, following the proportions for leaves. Bring to a boil over medium-high heat, reduce the heat to medium, and gently boil for 15 to 20 minutes. Strain into cups and add sweeteners or lemon to taste.

Hot Mulled Cider

Great on frosty mornings—especially with *Beignets* (page 60) or warm muffins.

6 cups apple or cherry cider
1/4 cup packed brown sugar, or to taste
1 cinnamon stick
5 or 6 whole cloves
5 or 6 whole allspice
Zest of 1 lemon or orange, cut into julienne

In a saucepan, combine all of the ingredients and place over medium heat, stirring until the sugar dissolves. Bring just to the boiling point, then reduce the heat to low, cover, and simmer to blend the flavors, about 10 minutes. Strain and serve.

Makes 6 servings.

Mexican Hot Cocoa

This spicy hot drink is popular throughout Mexico.

$1/4$ **cup unsweetened cocoa powder**
$1/4$ **cup packed brown sugar**
1 cinnamon stick
3 or 4 whole cloves
Salt
3 cups milk
3 teaspoons pure vanilla extract
Cinnamon sticks for stirring (optional)

In a saucepan, combine the cocoa, brown sugar, 1 cup water, cinnamon stick, cloves, and a pinch of salt and place over medium heat. Bring to a boil, reduce the heat to low, and simmer for about 5 minutes.

Stirring constantly with a wire whisk or wooden spoon, add the milk to the hot cocoa. Heat until just under the boiling point, then remove from the heat and stir in the vanilla. Strain to remove the cinnamon stick and cloves. Transfer to a blender or use a hand mixer or whisk and blend until foamy. Serve piping hot, with cinnamon sticks for stirring (if using).

Makes 4 servings.

French Hot Chocolate

Reserve this rich cup for those special mornings of overindulgence.

2 ounces (2 squares) unsweetened baking chocolate, broken or chopped
3 ounces (3 squares) finest-quality bittersweet or semisweet chocolate, broken or chopped
$1/2$ **cup sugar**
$2^1/2$ **cups milk**
2 cups light cream, half and half, or heavy (whipping) cream
$3/4$ **teaspoon pure vanilla extract**

In a saucepan, combine the chocolates, sugar, milk, and cream and place over medium heat. Stir frequently with a wire whisk or wooden spoon until the chocolate melts and the sugar dissolves. Heat until just under the boiling point, then remove from the heat and beat in a blender or with a rotary beater until smooth and frothy. Stir in the vanilla and serve hot.

Berry Refresher

Add this change-of-pace juice to your summer breakfast table.

4 cups fresh strawberries or raspberries, or a combination
2 cups freshly squeezed apple or orange juice
1/4 cup freshly squeezed lemon or lime juice
Sugar
Fresh mint for garnish

In a blender, combine the berries, juices, and sugar to taste and mix until very smooth. Strain if you wish. Chill, or serve over a little crushed ice. Garnish each glass with a sprig of mint.

Makes 4 servings.

Sparkling Citrus Blend

Although nutritionally it's better to eat the whole fruit, most of us love morning juices, especially freshly squeezed. They can, however, be a shock to the system, and most nutritionists advise diluting the juice; I enjoy adding sparkling water to freshly extracted juice. In this refreshing blend, the mixed juices can be held covered in the refrigerator for a short time before serving. Stir in the sparkling water or wine at the last minute.

3 cups freshly squeezed orange juice
1 cup freshly squeezed pink grapefruit juice
1/4 cup freshly squeezed lemon juice
About 2 cups sparkling water or sparkling wine
Slices or wedges of one of the fruits for garnish

In a pitcher, combine the juices and mix until well blended. Quickly stir in the sparkling water or wine, pour into glasses, garnish with fresh fruit, and serve immediately.

Makes 4 servings.

Bellini

Harry's Bar in Venice introduced this sparkling eye-opener in the 1930s. When white peaches are in season, peel and stone ripe fruits and put them through a food mill. If the peaches are not very sweet, add simple syrup to taste. Cover tightly and chill or freeze for later use. The puree is combined with Prosecco, an Italian dry sparkling wine; substitute fruitier Spumante or a dry domestic sparkling wine if you can't locate Prosecco.

1 cup white peach puree, well chilled
1 bottle (750ml) Prosecco, well chilled

Fill fluted champagne or tall highball glasses with ice and let stand until the glasses are chilled, then discard the ice. For each Bellini, in a cocktail shaker, combine 1 ounce of the chilled peach puree and 3 ounces of the sparkling wine and gently shake to blend. Pour into a cold glass and serve immediately.

Makes 8 servings.

Mimosa

This old favorite always adds sparkle to any special breakfast.

3 cups freshly squeezed orange juice, well chilled
1 bottle (750 ml) brut champagne or other dry sparkling wine,
 well chilled
Fresh mint leaves or borage flowers for garnish

For each Mimosa, pour 1/4 cup orange juice into a fluted champagne glass. Slowly add 2 ounces champagne, stir gently, garnish with mint or borage, and serve immediately.

Makes 12 servings.

Bloody Mary

In some circles, this morning classic has become almost as American as bacon and eggs. Teetotalers can enjoy the spicy drink sans spirits.

3 cups chilled tomato juice
$1/3$ cup freshly squeezed lemon juice
1 tablespoon prepared horseradish
$1^1/2$ teaspoons Worcestershire sauce, or to taste
Salt
Freshly ground black pepper
Hot sauce
1 cup chilled vodka
Fresh inner celery stalks with leaves for garnish

In a blender or cocktail shaker, combine the tomato juice, lemon juice, horseradish, Worcestershire sauce, and salt, pepper, and hot sauce to taste and mix thoroughly. Stir in the vodka and pour into 4 ice-filled glasses. Garnish with celery.

Makes 4 servings.

Ramos Fizz

Tradition has it that this drink was invented in New Orleans in the 1880s.

$3/4$ cup gin
$3/4$ cup sweet and sour drink mixer
$1^1/2$ cups light cream, half and half, or heavy (whipping) cream
6 tablespoons Curaçao or other orange-flavored liqueur
Juice of $1/2$ lime
4 egg whites
1 cup crushed ice
Powdered sugar
Freshly grated nutmeg

In a blender, combine all of the ingredients, including powdered sugar and nutmeg to taste, and blend until thick. Divide equally among 4 tall chilled glasses.

Makes 4 servings.

Yogurt Smoothy

Nutritious breakfasts-in-a-glass are good alternatives for those hurried mornings.

1 cup plain yogurt
1 cup crushed ice
2 cups chopped fresh fruit, one kind or a combination
Sugar
Vanilla or almond extract (optional)

In a blender, combine all of the ingredients, including sugar and vanilla or almond extract (if using) to taste, and puree until smooth. Serve immediately.

Makes 2 servings.

Breakfast Bahia

My friend Lenny Meyer and I often enjoyed this quick liquid breakfast during our hectic years in New York City.

1 cup milk
$2/3$ cup freshly squeezed orange juice
$2/3$ cup pineapple juice
$1/3$ cup cream of coconut (available wherever drink mixers are sold)
$1/2$ teaspoon coconut extract
1 banana
2 eggs (optional)
3 ice cubes
Fresh pineapple for garnish

In a blender, combine all of the ingredients except the fresh pineapple and blend until liquefied. Pour into chilled glasses, garnish with fresh pineapple, and serve immediately.

Makes 2 servings.

Fresh Fruits

Whether served alone, mixed together in seasonal compotes, or artfully combined on individual plates, luscious fruit is one of the most welcomed pleasures of any morning meal. For optimal flavor, always choose whatever is in its natural season—not forced to meet supermarket demands. Ripen the fruit to perfection before serving it chilled or at room temperature, according to your preference. When combining, choose compatible fruits. (I have a prejudice against mixing crisp apples with soft fruits and prefer using them on their own.) Here are a few ideas to stimulate your imagination.

Slice bananas, preferably red or other stubby varieties, into individual bowls and top with lightly sweetened heavy cream; sprinkle with toasted nuts for a change of pace.

Serve whole, quartered, or sliced figs with lightly sweetened cream; peel green figs, leave black types intact.

Marinate mixed soft fruits or mixed citrus in freshly squeezed orange juice and a little lemon juice; garnish with fresh pomegranate seeds when in season.

Generously sprinkle mixed melon balls or cubes with chopped fresh mint. If desired, add a splash of champagne just before serving.

Combine several types of summer berries and serve with a dollop of crème fraîche, plain or vanilla yogurt, or a berry sorbet.

Combine sliced papaya, pineapple, mango, bananas, or other tropical fruits, then add a splash of rum or pineapple juice and sprinkle with freshly grated coconut and/or minced crystallized ginger.

Stand thin slices of peeled cantaloupe or other melon (except watermelon) upright in a basket or bowl and fill the center with fresh berries.

Berry Butter

During berry season, stir up this quick treat to spread on muffins, toast, or pancakes. In other seasons, use frozen berries.

$1/2$ cup (1 stick) unsalted butter, at room temperature
1 cup fresh berries or thawed and drained frozen berries
$1/4$ cup powdered sugar, or to taste

In a food processor, blend the butter until smooth. Add the berries and sugar and blend well. Transfer to a bowl, cover, and refrigerate for up to 1 week. Return to room temperature shortly before serving.

Makes about 1 cup.

and serve immediately. Alternatively, store in the freezer for up to several weeks, then place in the refrigerator to soften for about 1 hour before serving.

Makes 6 servings.

Apple Butter

You can also use this technique with blueberries, pears, nectarines, peaches, plums, or strawberries. I prefer the intense taste of the fruit alone, but you may choose to add ground cinnamon and cloves to taste when you add the sweetener.

8 tart apples (about 2 pounds), peeled, cored, and coarsely chopped
1 cup unfiltered apple juice or cider
About $1^2/_3$ cups packed brown sugar or honey
Grated zest and juice of 1 lemon

In a heavy saucepan, combine the apples and the juice or cider and place over medium heat. Cook, stirring frequently, until the fruit is soft and the liquid has evaporated, about 10 minutes. Transfer to a food processor or blender and puree until smooth, or put through a food mill or strainer. Measure the puree into a heavy saucepan and add about $1/_3$ cup brown sugar or honey, or to taste, for each cup of apple puree. Cook over *very* low heat, stirring occasionally, until very thick and dark brown, from 2 to 4 hours.

Pack into sterilized jars, cover, and refrigerate for up to several weeks. Alternatively, pack into hot, sterilized canning jars and seal tightly following the canning-jar manufacturer's instructions. Check the jars and store those with proper seals in a cool place for up to 1 year. Any jar that does not have a proper seal should be refrigerated as above.

Makes about 5 cups.

Morning Sorbets

Instead of juice, begin a hot-weather morning with a slushy fruit concoction that's eaten with a spoon. Puree the fruits in a food processor or blender.

1 cup sugar
4 cups pureed fresh berries or melon; or pureed poached nectarines,
**   peaches, or pears; or freshly squeezed juice**
Fresh mint leaves or edible flowers for garnish

In a saucepan, combine the sugar and 1 cup water over high heat and boil until the sugar dissolves. Remove from the heat and cool completely.

Add the cold sugar syrup to taste to the pureed fruit. Freeze in an ice cream maker or sorbet machine according to the manufacturer's directions. Spoon into chilled dishes, garnish with mint or flowers,

Egyptian Spiced Winter Fruits
(Koschaf)

Serve in bowls, with plenty of the spicy poaching syrup.

1¹/₂ cups dried figs, preferably white, stems removed
1¹/₂ cups pitted prunes
1¹/₂ cups dried apricots, nectarines, or pears, preferably
    unsulphured
³/₄ cup golden raisins
1 lemon, preferably Meyer variety, thinly sliced, then cut into half
    circles
2 cinnamon sticks
¹/₂ cup sugar, or to taste
¹/₂ cup pine nuts
¹/₃ cup freshly squeezed lemon juice
Heavy (whipping) cream for passing (optional)

In a large saucepan, combine the figs with warm water to cover. Soak
for 1 hour, then drain. Add enough fresh water to cover the figs by
3 inches, place over medium heat, and simmer until just soft, 5 to 10
minutes, then add the prunes, apricots or other fruits, raisins, sliced
lemon, cinnamon sticks, and sugar and simmer over low heat, stirring
gently, until the sugar dissolves, about 5 minutes.

Remove the fruit from the heat. Stir in the pine nuts, lemon juice,
and enough water to cover the fruit by 3 inches. Cover and refrigerate
for several days to allow the fruits to absorb the liquid and develop
flavor.

Serve chilled, at room temperature, or warmed. Pass the cream for
drizzling over the top (if using).

Makes 8 servings.

Baked Stuffed Apples

Select good baking apples such as Baldwin, Courtland, or Golden
Delicious.

4 large firm baking apples
3 tablespoons dried currants or raisins
2 tablespoons light brown sugar
2 tablespoons unsalted butter, melted
2 teaspoons freshly squeezed lemon juice
1 teaspoon ground cinnamon
¹/₄ cup Granola (page 22)
1 cup apple juice or cider, preferably unfiltered
Heavy (whipping) cream, light cream, or half and half for serving

Preheat an oven to 350° F.

Core the apples, being careful not to go all the way through to the
bottoms, and remove about ¹/₂ inch of the peel around the top of each
apple. Trim the bottoms if necessary to stand the apples upright, and
place the apples in a small baking dish.

Combine the currants or raisins, 1 tablespoon of the brown sugar,
1 tablespoon of the melted butter, the lemon juice, and the cinnamon
in a bowl. Stir well, and then spoon the filling equally into the
hollowed cores of the apples. Sprinkle with the granola.

In a small bowl, combine the apple juice or cider with the remaining
1 tablespoon brown sugar and 1 tablespoon melted butter and blend
well. Pour the mixture over the apples. Cover with a lid or aluminum
foil and bake for 30 minutes. Uncover and bake, basting frequently
with the pan juices, until the apples are tender when pierced, about
30 minutes longer.

Serve warm or at room temperature. Pass a pitcher of cream to pour
over the apples at the table.

Makes 4 servings.

Fig Preserves

Among my fondest childhood memories are the hours spent in a fig tree across the levee from the Baptist parsonage where we lived. Even though the Little River has long since claimed that tree, the fig preserves that my mother makes and sends me every year whisk me back to those carefree days. I never get enough. Our family friend, "Miss Carrie" Smith, who lived to be almost a hundred, first showed us how to make these delectables.

Ripe fresh figs
Sugar

Peel the figs carefully, removing as little pulp as possible and retaining their natural shape. Measure the figs and place them in one layer in the bottom of a heavy pot. Pour on an equal measure of sugar. Add about 1 cup water for every 2 cups of figs and shake the pot until the figs are covered with sugar. Place over very low heat and cook until the sugar melts. Increase the heat to medium and cook just until the figs are clear and the liquid bubbles to a thick syrupy consistency, about 45 to 55 minutes.

Remove from the heat, cover the pot, and let stand overnight at room temperature.

Pack the figs into sterilized jars, cover, and refrigerate for up to several weeks. Alternatively, reheat the figs, pack into hot, sterilized canning jars, and seal tightly following the canning-jar manufacturer's instructions. Check the jars and store those with proper seals in a cool place for up to 1 year. Any jar that does not have a proper seal should be refrigerated as above.

Fruit Jam

Follow this same procedure with any whole berries or chopped summer fruits such as apricots, peaches, or pitted cherries. The cooking time will vary according to the type of fruit and the degree of ripeness.

Fresh berries or chopped fruit
Sugar

Measure the berries or chopped fruit and place them in a heavy pan, crushing some of the fruit with the back of a wooden spoon to release the juices. Place over low heat and cook until the fruit is soft, 5 to 10 minutes. Then, for each cup of fruit, add 3/4 to 1 cup sugar, according to taste, and stir constantly until the sugar dissolves. Increase the heat to medium and bring the fruit to a boil, stirring constantly to prevent sticking. Cook until the mixture is thick, about 15 minutes. When a teaspoonful of the jam dropped onto a cold plate holds together, remove the pan from the heat. Avoid overcooking since the jam will continue to thicken as it cools.

Store as directed in the adjacent recipe for fig preserves.

Lemon or Lime Curd

This tangy spread does wonderful things to warm muffins and grain-rich loaf breads such as the Oatmeal Loaf on page 28. For a lighter curd texture, substitute 4 whole eggs for an equal number of yolks. I prefer curd without flecks of zest, so I strain the zest out after it contributes the zing. If you wish, wait and add the zest after the curd is strained.

6 egg yolks
1 1/4 cups sugar
Pinch of salt
3/4 cup freshly squeezed lemon or lime juice
1 1/2 tablespoons minced or grated fresh lemon or lime zest
1/2 cup (1 stick) unsalted butter, cut into small pieces

In a heavy noncorrosive pan, such as stainless steel, or in the top of a double boiler, combine the egg yolks, sugar, and salt and beat until light and well blended. Stir in the lemon or lime juice and zest. Add the butter and place over medium-low heat or over simmering water and cook, stirring and scraping the bottom of the pan constantly, until the mixture is thick enough to coat the back of a wooden spoon but remains pourable, about 10 minutes over direct heat or about 15 minutes over simmering water. To prevent the eggs from curdling, do not allow the mixture to approach a boil.

Strain the curd through a fine mesh sieve into a bowl; discard the residue from the sieve. Immediately place a layer of plastic wrap directly on the top of the curd to prevent a skin from forming. Set aside to cool completely, then discard the plastic wrap, cover tightly, and refrigerate for up to 3 weeks.

Makes about 2 cups.

GRAINS

Granola

Most commercial granolas are coated with oil or butter and heavily sweetened with honey. Try this version for a reduced-calorie, high-energy breakfast or snack. Store in tightly sealed plastic bags or glass jars in a cool place.

2 1/2 cups regular (not instant) rolled oats
2 tablespoons whole wheat flour
3 tablespoons nonfat dry milk
1/3 cup sesame seeds
1/2 cup sunflower seeds
1/2 cup chopped almonds
2 teaspoons grated or minced fresh lemon or orange zest
1 tablespoon ground cinnamon
1/3 cup thawed frozen unsweetened apple juice concentrate
1/2 cup hot water
1/2 cup chopped dates or granulated date sugar (available in
     natural-foods stores)
1/2 cup dried currants

Preheat an oven to 300° F.

In a large bowl, combine the oats, flour, dry milk, sesame and sunflower seeds, almonds, lemon or orange zest, and ground cinnamon and mix well. Add the apple juice concentrate and hot water and mix thoroughly.

In shallow baking pans, thinly spread the mixture and bake, stirring every 10 minutes, until dry and toasted, about 45 minutes. Pour into a large mixing bowl and cool slightly before stirring in the chopped dates and the currants. Let cool completely before storing in an airtight container.

Makes about 5 cups.

Swiss Cold Oat Cereal

Prepare and refrigerate this healthy mixture the night before.

1 1/3 cups regular (not instant) rolled oats
2 cups freshly squeezed orange juice or water
2 teaspoons freshly squeezed lemon juice
3/4 cup chopped almonds
2 apples, grated, or 2 cups fresh berries, sliced fresh fruits, or
     reconstituted dried fruits
1/4 cup toasted sunflower seeds (optional)
Plain yogurt, milk, or cream for serving
Honey or sugar for serving

In a bowl, combine the oats and orange juice or water, cover, and refrigerate overnight to soften the oats.

Just before serving, stir in the lemon juice, almonds, apples or other fruit, and sunflower seeds (if using). Spoon into individual serving bowls. Pass the yogurt, milk, or cream and the sweetener at the table.

Makes 4 servings.

Hot Multi-Grain Cereal

Several brands of mixed-grain cereals are available for quickly cooking into cold-day treats. Here's how to mix up your own grains, then store them for cooking as needed. The amounts can be varied according to taste and availability. Both packaged mixed-grain cereals and the individual dried grains can be found in natural-foods stores and some supermarkets.

CEREAL MIX
1 cup dried hominy
1 cup rye or triticale berries
1 cup brown rice
1 cup millet
1 cup pearled barley
1 cup steel-cut oats, sometimes sold as Scotch oats
1 cup bulgur (precooked cracked wheat)
1 cup sesame seeds

4 cups water, milk, or apple juice
1 teaspoon salt, or to taste
1 teaspoon ground cinnamon
$1/4$ cup raisins
Brown sugar or pure maple syrup for serving
Milk or cream, warmed, for serving

To prepare the Cereal Mix, place the hominy, rye or triticale berries, brown rice, millet, and barley, separately or in combination, in a food processor and pulse quickly to crack them into small pieces. Transfer to a large bowl. Add the oats, bulgur, and sesame seeds and mix thoroughly. Store in airtight containers in a cool place or in the refrigerator.

To cook, in a saucepan, bring the water, milk, or apple juice to a boil over medium-high heat. Stir in 1 cup of the cereal mix, the salt, cinnamon, and raisins and cook, stirring frequently, until the grains are tender, 7 to 10 minutes. Spoon into bowls. Pass the sugar or syrup and milk or cream at the table.

Makes 8 cups cereal mix; each cup makes 2 servings.

Fruity Oatmeal

A perfect rib-sticking start for a wintry day.

2 cups milk
2 cups regular (not instant) rolled oats
$1/2$ teaspoon salt
$3/4$ cup chopped pitted prunes or raisins
2 apples or firm pears, shredded
Ground cinnamon
Milk or cream, warmed, for serving
Brown sugar for serving

In a heavy saucepan, combine 2 cups water, the milk, oats, and salt and place over medium-high heat. Bring to a boil, cover, reduce the heat to achieve a simmer, and cook for 5 minutes. Stir in the prunes or raisins, apples or pears, and cinnamon to taste and continue to simmer, stirring frequently, until tender, about 5 minutes more. Spoon into bowls. Pass milk or cream and sugar at the table.

Makes 4 servings.

Berry Muffins with Nutmeg Sugar

Vary blueberries and cranberries according to the season.

1¹/₂ cups all-purpose flour
2 teaspoons baking powder
¹/₄ teaspoon salt
1 teaspoon ground cinnamon
¹/₂ teaspoon freshly grated nutmeg
2 eggs, at room temperature
¹/₃ cup sugar
3 tablespoons pure maple syrup
1 cup milk (not nonfat)
¹/₄ cup canola or other high-quality vegetable oil
1¹/₂ cups fresh blueberries or coarsely chopped cranberries
1 tablespoon sugar mixed with 1 teaspoon freshly grated nutmeg

Preheat an oven to 400° F. Grease twelve 3-inch muffin tins and set aside.

In a bowl, combine the flour, baking powder, salt, cinnamon, and nutmeg and stir to blend well. Set aside.

In another bowl, beat the eggs. Add the sugar, syrup, milk, and oil and mix well. Add the flour mixture and stir until the ingredients are just blended, then fold in the berries. Spoon into the prepared tins, filling each about three-quarters full. Sprinkle the tops with the nutmeg sugar. Bake until the muffins are lightly browned and a wooden skewer inserted in the center of a muffin comes out clean, about 20 minutes. Remove immediately from the tins and cool briefly on a wire rack before serving.

Makes 12 muffins.

Bran Muffins

I never tire of these dark, moist, and nutritious delights.

1¹/₂ cups unprocessed wheat or oat bran flakes, or a combination
1 cup dried currants or raisins
¹/₄ cup molasses
¹/₄ cup honey
1 cup buttermilk
2 eggs, at room temperature
¹/₂ cup canola or other high-quality vegetable oil
1 teaspoon pure vanilla extract
³/₄ cup all-purpose flour
¹/₄ cup whole wheat flour
1¹/₂ teaspoons baking powder
¹/₂ teaspoon baking soda
1¹/₂ teaspoons ground cinnamon
¹/₂ teaspoon freshly grated nutmeg
¹/₂ teaspoon ground allspice

In a bowl, combine the bran flakes, currants or raisins, molasses, honey, buttermilk, eggs, oil, and vanilla, and mix well. Set aside to soften the bran, at least 20 minutes, or cover and refrigerate for up to overnight.

Preheat an oven to 425° F. Grease twelve 3-inch muffin tins and set aside.

In a bowl, combine the flours, baking powder, baking soda, cinnamon, nutmeg, and allspice and blend well. Add to the moist bran mixture and stir until the ingredients are just blended. Spoon into the prepared tins, filling each about three-quarters full. Bake until a wooden skewer inserted in the center of a muffin comes out clean, 15 to 20 minutes. Remove immediately from the tins and cool briefly on a wire rack before serving.

Makes 12 muffins.

Fresh Apple Muffins

This batter can also be doubled and baked in a loaf pan or cake pan.

1¹/₂ cups all-purpose flour
2 teaspoons baking powder
¹/₂ teaspoon salt
1 cup sugar
³/₄ cup canola or other high-quality vegetable oil
¹/₂ cup milk (not nonfat)
2 eggs, at room temperature
1 teaspoon pure vanilla extract
1¹/₂ cups peeled and chopped apple
¹/₂ cup chopped pecans or walnuts

Preheat an oven to 350° F. Grease twelve 3-inch muffin tins and set aside.

In a bowl, combine the flour, baking powder, and salt and stir to blend well. Set aside.

In another bowl, combine the sugar, oil, milk, eggs, and vanilla and beat until creamy smooth. Add the flour mixture and stir until the ingredients are just blended, then fold in the apple and nuts. Spoon into the prepared tins, filling each about three-quarters full. Bake until a wooden skewer inserted in the center of a muffin comes out clean, about 25 minutes. Remove immediately from the tins and cool briefly on a wire rack before serving.

Makes 12 muffins.

Orange-Glazed Prune Muffins

Cook the prunes the night before for a quick morning sensation.

20 pitted prunes
1¹/₄ cups all-purpose flour
1 teaspoon baking powder
¹/₂ teaspoon baking soda
¹/₄ teaspoon salt
1 teaspoon freshly grated nutmeg
1 teaspoon ground cinnamon
¹/₂ teaspoon ground allspice
¹/₂ teaspoon ground cloves
¹/₂ cup canola or other high-quality vegetable oil
¹/₂ cup sugar
2 eggs, at room temperature
³/₄ cup buttermilk
¹/₂ cup chopped pecans or walnuts (optional)

ORANGE GLAZE
³/₄ cup powdered sugar
2 tablespoons freshly squeezed orange juice
1 tablespoon grated or minced fresh orange zest

In a saucepan, combine the prunes with enough water to cover by 3 inches and place over medium heat. Cook until soft, about 10 minutes. Drain, mash well, measure out 1 cup, and set aside.

Preheat an oven to 375° F. Grease twelve 3-inch muffin tins and set aside.

In a bowl, combine the flour, baking powder, baking soda, salt, nutmeg, cinnamon, allspice, and cloves and stir to blend well. Set aside.

In another bowl, combine the oil, sugar, eggs, and buttermilk and beat until well blended. Add the flour mixture and stir until the ingredients are just blended, then stir in the mashed prunes and nuts (if using). Spoon into the prepared tins, filling each about three-quarters full. Bake until the tops are browned and a wooden skewer inserted in the center of a muffin comes out clean, about 20 minutes. Remove immediately from the tins and cool briefly on a wire rack.

Meanwhile, to make the Orange Glaze, in a small bowl, combine all of the glaze ingredients and mix well. Brush the tops of the warm muffins with the glaze and serve warm.

Makes 12 muffins.

Spicy Cocoa Muffins

Inspired by Mexican Hot Cocoa (page 11), these are guaranteed to bring chocolate lovers to the breakfast table.

1¾ **cups all-purpose flour**
¾ **cup sugar**
6 **tablespoons unsweetened cocoa powder**
2 **teaspoons baking powder**
½ **teaspoon baking soda**
2 **teaspoons ground cinnamon**
¼ **teaspoon ground cloves**
¾ **teaspoon salt**
2 **eggs, at room temperature**
1 **cup buttermilk**
½ **cup (1 stick) unsalted butter, melted and cooled**
½ **cup finely chopped pecans or walnuts**
½ **cup semisweet chocolate chips**

Preheat an oven to 400° F. Grease twelve 3-inch muffin tins and set aside. In a bowl, combine the flour, sugar, cocoa powder, baking powder, baking soda, cinnamon, cloves, and salt and stir to blend well. Set aside.

In another bowl, combine the eggs, buttermilk, and melted butter and beat well. Add the flour mixture and stir until the ingredients are just blended, then fold in the nuts and chocolate chips. Spoon the mixture into the prepared tins, filling each about three-quarters full. Bake until a wooden skewer inserted in the center of a muffin comes out clean, about 15 minutes. Remove immediately from the tins and cool briefly on a wire rack.

Makes 12 muffins.

Popovers

For maximum puffiness, avoid opening the oven door until the popovers are almost done. Serve piping hot with plenty of butter and jam or honey.

3 **tablespoons unsalted butter, melted and cooled**
4 **eggs, at room temperature**
1⅓ **cups milk (not nonfat)**
1⅓ **cups all-purpose flour**
1 **tablespoon sugar**
½ **teaspoon salt**

Preheat an oven to 425° F. Generously butter eight 6-ounce custard cups and set aside.

In a blender, combine all of the ingredients and blend until smooth. Divide the batter evenly among the prepared custard cups. Place on a baking sheet, leaving space around each cup for hot air to circulate. Bake until well puffed and firm to the touch, about 25 minutes, then reduce the heat to 350° F and bake until browned, about 15 minutes longer. Transfer to a work surface, run a dull knife blade around the inside of each cup to loosen, remove the popovers, and serve immediately.

Makes 8 popovers.

Oatmeal Loaf

Try this quick bread with Apple Butter (page 17) or Lemon or Lime Curd (page 20).

$1^1/_2$ cups regular (not instant) rolled oats
$1^1/_2$ cups buttermilk
$^3/_4$ cup whole wheat flour
$^3/_4$ cup all-purpose flour
$^3/_4$ teaspoon salt
$1^1/_2$ teaspoons ground ginger
$^3/_4$ teaspoon freshly grated nutmeg
$2^1/_2$ teaspoons baking powder
$^1/_2$ teaspoon baking soda
$^1/_3$ cup canola or other high-quality vegetable oil
$^1/_3$ cup pure maple syrup
2 eggs, at room temperature
1 cup golden raisins

In a bowl, combine the oats and buttermilk and let stand to soften the oats, about 30 minutes.

Preheat an oven to 350° F. Grease and flour a 9-by-5-inch loaf pan and set aside.

In another bowl, combine the flours, salt, ginger, nutmeg, baking powder, and baking soda and stir to blend well. Set aside.

Add the oil, syrup, and eggs to the soaked oats and mix well. Add the flour mixture and stir until the ingredients are just blended, then stir in the raisins. Spoon into the prepared pan. Bake until a wooden skewer inserted in the center comes out clean, about 1 hour. Transfer to a wire rack to cool for about 10 minutes, then turn out onto the rack to cool a few minutes longer. Serve warm or at room temperature.

Makes 1 loaf.

Whole Wheat Zucchini Bread

Since this bread keeps for two weeks or longer in the refrigerator and freezes nicely for longer storage, you may wish to multiply the recipe when zucchini is plentiful.

$^3/_4$ cup all-purpose flour
$^1/_2$ cup whole wheat pastry flour
$^1/_2$ teaspoon baking soda
$^1/_4$ teaspoon baking powder
$^1/_2$ teaspoon salt
1 teaspoon ground cinnamon
2 eggs, at room temperature
$^1/_2$ cup canola or other high-quality vegetable oil
3 tablespoons molasses
$^1/_2$ cup packed light brown sugar
1 teaspoon pure vanilla extract
1 cup shredded zucchini, drained if watery
$^1/_2$ cup dried currants or raisins
$^1/_2$ cup chopped nuts

Preheat an oven to 350° F. Grease and flour a 9-by-5-inch loaf pan and set aside.

In a bowl, combine the flours, baking soda, baking powder, salt, and cinnamon and stir to blend well. Set aside.

In another bowl, combine the eggs, oil, molasses, sugar, and vanilla, and beat until thick and smooth. Add the flour mixture and stir until the ingredients are just blended, then fold in the zucchini, currants or raisins, and nuts. Spoon into the prepared pan. Bake until a wooden skewer inserted in the center comes out clean, about 1 hour. Transfer to a wire rack to cool for about 10 minutes, then turn out onto the rack to cool a few minutes longer. Serve warm or at room temperature.

Makes 1 loaf.

Buttermilk Biscuits

My aunt, Doris Keith, of Jackson, Mississippi, makes a pan of wonderful hot biscuits almost every morning. Her recipe is very simple; the perfection she exhibits probably comes from the daily practice. While my aunt recommends self-rising flour (which already contains baking powder and salt), I've adapted her recipe to all-purpose flour.

As a youngster, I always asked for "white" biscuits, which meant cooked only until the tops were barely beginning to brown. I still like them this way. If you prefer a browner top, brush the biscuits with melted butter before baking. If you enjoy the sides crusty, arrange the biscuits about 1 inch apart in the baking pan; for soft sides, arrange them touching.

2 cups all-purpose flour
2 teaspoons baking powder
1/2 teaspoon baking soda
1/2 teaspoon salt
1/2 cup solid vegetable shortening
3/4 cup buttermilk

Preheat an oven to 400° F. Lightly grease a baking sheet and set aside.

In a bowl or food processor, combine the flour, baking powder, baking soda, and salt. Cut in the shortening with your fingertips, a pastry blender, or the steel blade until the mixture resembles coarse cornmeal. If using a food processor, transfer the mixture to a bowl. Add the buttermilk and stir just until the mixture sticks together.

Turn the dough out onto a lightly floured surface and knead lightly and quickly, about 30 seconds. Roll out with a lightly floured rolling pin to about 1/2 inch thick. Cut with a floured 2 1/2-inch round biscuit cutter. Place close together on the prepared sheet. Bake until lightly browned, 10 to 12 minutes. Serve piping hot with butter and good jelly, jam, honey, or syrup.

Makes about 12 biscuits.

Yeast Biscuits

These light biscuits were very popular in my hometown. I've kept the recipe through the years and have enjoyed serving them from coast to coast. Serve piping hot with plenty of butter and good jelly or jam. The dough keeps in the refrigerator for several days. Cut off and roll out only what you need at one time.

1 package (1/4 ounce) quick-rising active dry yeast
5 tablespoons warm water (110° to 115° F)
5 cups all-purpose flour
5 teaspoons baking powder
1/2 teaspoon baking soda
3 tablespoons sugar
1 teaspoon salt
1 cup canola or other high-quality vegetable oil
2 cups buttermilk

In a small bowl, sprinkle the yeast over the water, stir to dissolve, and let stand until soft and foamy, about 5 minutes. (Discard the mixture and start over with a fresh package of yeast if bubbles have not formed within 5 minutes.)

In a bowl or food processor, combine the flour, baking powder, baking soda, sugar, and salt. Cut the oil into the mixture with a pastry blender or the steel blade until the mixture is the texture of coarse cornmeal. If using a food processor, transfer the mixture to a bowl. Pour in the buttermilk and softened yeast. Stir the mixture quickly to combine the liquid with the dry ingredients. Cover and refrigerate for at least 1 hour, or preferably overnight.

Lightly grease baking sheets and set aside.

Form the chilled dough into a ball and turn out onto a generously floured surface. Knead lightly and quickly, about 1 minute. Roll out with a lightly floured rolling pin to about 1/2 inch thick. Cut with a floured 2 1/2-inch round cutter and place barely touching on the prepared sheets. Cover with a kitchen towel and set aside to rise just until puffy, 20 to 30 minutes.

Preheat an oven to 400° F. Bake until lightly browned, 10 to 15 minutes.

Makes about 48 biscuits.

Scones with Orange Butter

These butter-rich British biscuits, shown on the back cover, are traditionally served with afternoon tea, but they are equally comforting in the morning.

ORANGE BUTTER
2 tablespoons grated or minced fresh orange zest
3 tablespoons powdered sugar
$1/2$ cup (1 stick) unsalted butter, softened

SCONES
2 cups all-purpose flour
3 tablespoons sugar
1 teaspoon baking powder
$1/2$ teaspoon baking soda
$1/2$ teaspoon salt
$1/2$ cup (1 stick) unsalted butter, chilled, cut into small pieces
$2/3$ cup buttermilk
$1/3$ cup dried currants
1 tablespoon grated or minced fresh lemon or orange zest
(optional)
Unsalted butter, melted, for brushing
Sugar for sprinkling

To make the Orange Butter, in a food processor, combine the orange zest, powdered sugar, and butter and blend until well mixed. Refrigerate until just before serving.

Preheat an oven to 350° F. Lightly grease a baking sheet and set aside.

To make the scones, in a bowl or food processor, combine the flour, sugar, baking powder, baking soda, and salt. Cut in the cold butter with your fingertips, a pastry blender, or the steel blade until the mixture resembles coarse cornmeal. If using a food processor, transfer the mixture to a bowl. Add the buttermilk, currants, and zest (if using) and stir just until the mixture sticks together.

Turn the dough out onto a lightly floured surface and knead lightly and quickly, about 30 seconds. Pat the dough into a ball and flatten it to form a disk, then roll out with a lightly floured rolling pin into a circle about $1/2$ inch thick. Using a floured knife, cut into 8 wedges, or use a floured metal cutter to form round or diamond shapes about

$2^{1}/2$ inches in diameter. Place on the prepared baking sheet, leaving space between each scone. Brush the tops with melted butter and sprinkle with sugar. Bake until golden brown, 20 to 25 minutes. Serve warm, with the reserved Orange Butter.

Makes 8 scones.

VARIATIONS: For whole-wheat scones, shown in the photograph above, substitute 1 cup whole-wheat pastry flour for 1 cup of the all-purpose flour. Sprinkle with a mixture of ground cinnamon and sugar.

Substitute raisins, dried cranberries or cherries, or chopped crystallized ginger for the currants.

Brioches

Here's an easy version of the French classic. In addition to serving them with butter and jam, you can split the brioches and fill with scrambled eggs or other favorite fillings. Be sure to use a heavy-duty mixer, as lighter models may overheat from the long kneading time.

1/2 cup warm water or whole milk (110° to 115° F)
5 tablespoons sugar
1 package (1/4 ounce) quick-rising active dry yeast
3 1/2 cups sifted all-purpose flour
3/4 cup (1 1/2 sticks) unsalted butter, at room temperature
4 eggs, at room temperature
1 teaspoon salt
1 teaspoon grated or minced fresh lemon zest (optional)
1 egg yolk beaten with 1 tablespoon milk for brushing

To make a sponge, in a small bowl, combine the water or milk and 1 tablespoon of the sugar, sprinkle with the yeast, stir to dissolve, and set aside until soft and foamy, about 5 minutes. (Discard the mixture and start over with a fresh package of yeast if bubbles have not formed within 5 minutes.) Stir in 1 cup of the flour and set aside to rise for 30 minutes.

In the bowl of a heavy-duty stand mixer fitted with a flat beater, beat the butter at medium speed until light and fluffy, about 45 seconds. Add the remaining 1/4 cup sugar, the eggs, salt, and lemon zest (if using) and mix at medium speed until as smooth as possible; the mixture may appear curdled. Add 1 cup of the remaining flour and beat at low speed until incorporated. With the mixer still running, continue adding flour, 1/2 cup at a time, stopping to scrape down the bowl and beater as necessary. Exchange the beater for a dough hook. Add the risen sponge mixture and knead at high speed until the dough is smooth and very elastic, 10 to 15 minutes. The dough should cling to the hook and make a slapping sound against the sides of the bowl, and the longer kneading insures the characteristic texture of brioche. Transfer the dough to a heavily buttered bowl, cover the bowl tightly with plastic wrap, and set aside in a warm place to rise until doubled in bulk, about 1 hour.

Generously butter 12 fluted and flared 3-inch brioche or regular muffin tins and set aside.

Punch the dough down. Pinch off about 3/4 cup of the dough and reserve. Divide the remaining dough into 12 equal pieces and shape each into a smooth round by pulling the surface of the dough to the underside of the round. Place the rounds, smooth side up, in the prepared tins, pressing lightly to fit the bottoms into the tins.

Divide the reserved dough into 12 pieces and shape with your hands into teardrop shapes. Poke a hole in the center of each dough round with your finger and firmly insert the small end of a teardrop-shaped dough piece. Cover with a kitchen towel and let stand in a warm place until almost doubled in bulk, about 25 minutes.

Preheat an oven to 375° F.

Gently brush the top of each brioche with the egg-milk mixture, being careful to avoid accumulation in the crease where the two pieces of dough are joined. Bake until richly browned, 18 to 20 minutes. Remove immediately from the tins and cool briefly on a wire rack. Serve warm.

Makes 12 brioches.

VARIATION: Instead of forming rounds, divide the dough into 2 pieces and place in 2 well-buttered 8 1/2-by-4 1/2-by-2 3/4-inch loaf pans. Let rise until the dough is about 1 inch from the top of the pans, then brush as directed and bake until richly browned, about 45 minutes. The rich loaf is excellent toasted, turned into ultra-rich French toast, or used for breakfast sandwiches of bacon and eggs or grilled ham and cheese.

Croissants

The technique for making these flaky French breakfast standbys is easy; it's the chilling between steps that makes the preparation a long one, and the several foldings of the dough that make the rolls flaky.

1/4 cup warm water (110° to 115° F)
3 tablespoons sugar
1 package (1/4 ounce) quick-rising active dry yeast
2²/₃ cups all-purpose flour
1¹/₂ teaspoons salt
1 cup whole milk
1 cup (2 sticks) unsalted butter, softened
1 egg beaten with 1 tablespoon water for brushing

In a small bowl, combine the warm water and 1 tablespoon of the sugar, sprinkle with the yeast, stir to dissolve, and let stand until soft and foamy, about 5 minutes. (Discard the mixture and start over with a fresh package of yeast if bubbles have not formed within 5 minutes.)

In a bowl, combine the remaining 2 tablespoons sugar, the flour, and salt and stir to blend well. Add the milk and foamy yeast mixture and stir until moistened, scraping down the sides of the bowl. The dough should be rather loose, much like unkneaded biscuit dough. Cover the bowl tightly with plastic wrap, and set aside at room temperature to relax the gluten for about 30 minutes, then refrigerate for at least 5 hours, or up to overnight.

Place the cold butter on a generously floured work surface. Using a rolling pin, pound the butter until softened, turning often to coat with the flour from the board, then roll the butter into a flat piece about 5 by 6 inches and set aside. (Refrigerate briefly if the butter begins to get warm; when ready to use it should be about the same temperature as the dough in the following step.)

Scrape up all traces of butter from the work surface and sprinkle lightly with flour. Turn out the chilled dough and roll it out into a rectangle about 8 by 12 inches, with the long side facing you. Place the butter with its short side facing you over the right half of the dough. Brush off excess flour from the dough, fold the left side over the buttered half, and press the edges together to seal. Press and roll

the folded dough out lengthwise to form a rectangle about 10 by 20 inches. Brushing off excess flour from the dough as you fold, bring the bottom third of the dough up over the middle third, then fold the top third down over it as you would a letter. Place on a baking sheet, cover with plastic wrap, and refrigerate for 45 minutes.

To "turn" the chilled dough, position it on a lightly floured surface with the long sealed side toward the right and roll it out into a rectangle about 10 by 20 inches. Again brushing off excess flour from the dough, fold it over in thirds as you would a letter. Place on a baking sheet, cover with plastic wrap, and refrigerate until well chilled, about 45 minutes.

Repeat the turning and chilling step 2 more times. After the final folding, refrigerate the dough for up to overnight.

Lightly grease 2 baking sheets and set aside.

On a lightly floured surface, roll out the dough into a 12-by-18-inch rectangle, lifting the dough to relax it and flouring the surface as needed. Using a sharp knife or pastry wheel, cut the dough lengthwise in half. Gently stretch 2 opposite corners of each piece to create diagonal edges, then cut each piece into 8 equal triangles with 4-inch bases. Hold each triangle by the wide end and pull towards the tip to stretch the dough while rolling it up from the wide end. Tuck the tip of the triangle slightly underneath the roll and curve the ends in toward the tip to form a crescent shape. Place about 2 inches apart on the prepared baking sheets. (At this point, the croissants can be covered and refrigerated overnight.) Lightly brush the tops and sides with the egg and water mixture, cover with a kitchen towel, and let rise in a warm place until almost doubled in size, 1 to 2 hours.

Preheat an oven to 425° F.

Gently brush the risen croissants again with the egg and water glaze. Bake for 10 minutes, then reduce the heat to 375° F and bake until golden brown, about 7 minutes longer. Transfer to wire racks to cool slightly before serving.

Makes 16 croissants.

Bagels

Bagels have become an American favorite, with bagel shops from coast to coast turning out the chewy rounds with a variety of flavors built in, or spread with almost any filling the imagination can dream up. My favorite way to eat them is split and toasted, smeared with cream cheese and dollops of jam. Cream cheese topped with lox, or smoked salmon, is a hallmark of Jewish cuisine. As an alternative, I often blend cream cheese with chopped smoked salmon and chives for spreading.

1¼ cups warm water (110° to 115° F)
2 teaspoons sugar
1 package (¼ ounce) quick-rising active dry yeast
¼ cup (½ stick) unsalted butter, melted and cooled, or solid
    vegetable shortening, at room temperature
1½ teaspoons salt
3 cups bread flour or all-purpose flour
1 egg beaten with 1 tablespoon water for brushing
Coarse salt or seeds (caraway, sesame, or poppy) for sprinkling
    (optional)

In a small bowl, combine the warm water and sugar, sprinkle with the yeast, stir to dissolve, and let stand until soft and foamy, about 5 minutes. (Discard the mixture and start over with a fresh package of yeast if bubbles have not formed within 5 minutes.)

In the bowl of a stand mixer fitted with a flat beater, combine the butter or shortening, salt, and foamy yeast mixture and beat at low speed until smooth. With the mixer still running, add the flour, ½ cup at a time, until incorporated. Exchange the beater for a dough hook. Knead at high speed, stopping to scrape down the bowl and hook as necessary, until the dough is smooth, elastic, and no longer sticky, about 5 minutes.

Gather the dough into a ball, transfer to a lightly buttered bowl, turn the dough to coat all sides with butter, cover the bowl tightly with plastic wrap, and let rise in a warm place until doubled in bulk, about 1 hour. (At this point, the dough can be punched down, covered, and refrigerated for up to overnight.)

Bring a large pot of water to a boil. Spread a kitchen towel alongside the stove top. Preheat an oven to 425° F. Lightly grease 2 large pizza screens or baking sheets and set aside.

Punch the dough down and turn it out onto a lightly floured surface. Divide it into 8 equal pieces and cover with a kitchen towel. Working with 1 piece of dough at a time, shape it into a smooth round by tightly pulling the surface of the dough to the underside and pinching together, repeating until a compact ball of dough is formed. Place, smooth side up, on the work surface and lightly press to flatten into a disk. Poke your index finger through the center to make a hole. Pick up the dough with your finger in the hole and insert your other index finger through the other side of the hole. Rotate your fingers around each other, stretching the dough to make a ring with an opening about 1½ inches in diameter. Set aside and repeat with the remaining dough pieces.

Drop the dough rings, a few at a time, into the boiling water. After the bagels float to the surface, cook for 2 minutes, then turn and cook until well puffed, light, and spongy, about 3 minutes longer. Using a slotted spoon, remove to the kitchen towel, smooth side up, to drain briefly.

When all the bagels have been boiled and drained, transfer them to the prepared screens or baking sheets, placing the bagels about 2 inches apart. Brush the tops with the egg and water mixture. Sprinkle with coarse salt or selected seeds (if using). Bake until lightly golden, about 15 minutes. Remove to wire racks to cool.

Makes 8 bagels.

VARIATIONS: For whole wheat bagels, substitute whole wheat flour for about one-third of the all-purpose flour; bake a few minutes longer.

To make egg bagels, add 3 beaten egg yolks along with the butter.

Butter-Rich Waffles

On those occasions when indulging is justified, try these delectable waffles that were a special favorite of my late good friend, Martha Jane Cotton. Although I like to cook waffles in a deep-pocketed Belgian waffle iron, any type of waffle iron will do. For a romantic change of pace, try the heart-shaped Scandinavian waffle maker. No matter what iron, be sure to season the grids according to the manufacturer's directions before adding the batter.

2 eggs, separated
1^1/$_2$ cups milk (not nonfat)
2 teaspoons baking powder
1 cup sifted all-purpose flour
^{1}/$_2$ cup (1 stick) unsalted butter, melted and cooled

Heat a waffle iron.

In a bowl, beat the egg whites until stiff but not dry. Reserve.

In another bowl, combine the egg yolks, milk, baking powder, flour, and melted butter and beat until smooth. Fold in the reserved egg whites. Bake until crisp according to directions on your waffle iron. Serve hot with your favorite toppings.

Makes 4 servings.

VARIATIONS: For a less rich version, reduce the amount of butter to ^{1}/$_4$ cup.

Add ^{1}/$_2$ to ^{3}/$_4$ cup chopped pecans or other nuts, toasted sunflower seeds, or crumbled bacon to the batter.

Substitute buttermilk, sour cream (not nonfat), or yogurt (not nonfat) for the milk. Reduce the baking powder to ^{1}/$_2$ teaspoon and add ^{1}/$_2$ teaspoon baking soda.

Tasty Toppings for Breakfast Treats

While the flavor of warm pure maple syrup is unsurpassable for drizzling over waffles, pancakes, and French toast, here are a few alternatives:

Jams, jellies, applesauce, fruit butters, honey, or fruit syrups.

Pureed seasonal fruit, plain or sweetened to taste with sugar, heated briefly in a saucepan or microwave oven.

Sliced apples, bananas, pears, or other fruits sautéed in a little butter until soft.

Cottage cheese pureed with fresh or cooked fruit.

Lightly whipped cream, crème fraîche, Mascarpone (Italian cream cheese), or yogurt.

Powdered sugar and a generous squeeze of fresh lemon or lime juice.

Warm chocolate sauce.

Buttermilk Pancakes

Although best when eaten immediately, pancakes may be kept in a warm oven for up to 15 minutes.

2 cups all-purpose flour
1 tablespoon sugar
1 teaspoon salt
1 teaspoon baking powder
1/2 teaspoon baking soda
1 1/2 cups buttermilk
1/2 to 1 cup milk (not nonfat)
2 eggs, at room temperature
1/4 cup (1/2 stick) unsalted butter, melted and cooled

In a bowl, combine the flour, sugar, salt, baking powder, and soda and stir to mix well. Set aside.

In another bowl, combine the buttermilk, 1/2 cup milk for thick pancakes or up to 1 cup milk for thinner pancakes, eggs, and butter and blend well. Add the flour mixture and stir until the ingredients are just blended.

Meanwhile, heat a nonstick griddle or large, heavy skillet over medium-high heat, then lightly brush with melted butter or oil or spray with oil.

Pour the batter, about 1/4 cup for each pancake, onto the cooking surface. Cook until the tops are bubbly, then turn and cook until the bottoms are browned. Serve hot with your favorite toppings.

Makes 4 to 6 servings.

VARIATIONS: Stir 1 cup chopped banana or other soft fruit or 1/2 cup chopped toasted nuts into the batter. Or sprinkle fresh blueberries or raspberries over the top after pouring onto the griddle.

Lemon Soufflé Pancakes

These light-as-air pancakes are a special treat.

6 eggs, separated
2 cups small-curd cottage or ricotta cheese (not nonfat)
1/4 cup canola or other high-quality vegetable oil
2 tablespoons sugar
1/2 teaspoon salt
4 teaspoons freshly squeezed lemon juice, preferably from Meyer variety
1 teaspoon grated or minced fresh lemon zest (optional)
4 teaspoons baking powder
1 cup all-purpose flour

In a bowl, beat the egg whites until stiff but not dry. Reserve.

In a food processor or blender, combine the egg yolks, cottage or ricotta cheese, oil, sugar, salt, lemon juice and zest (if using), baking powder, and flour and blend until smooth. Fold in the egg whites.

Meanwhile, heat a nonstick griddle or large, heavy skillet over medium-high heat, then lightly brush with melted butter or oil or spray with oil.

Pour the batter, about 1/4 cup for each pancake, onto the cooking surface. Cook until the tops are bubbly, then turn and cook until the bottoms are browned. Serve hot with your favorite toppings.

Makes 4 to 6 servings.

Round Danish Pancakes
(Aebleskiver)

Aebleskiver must be cooked in special pans that can be purchased at hardware or kitchenware stores. Serve with fruit jam, warm applesauce, honey, or syrup.

2 eggs, separated
2 cups buttermilk
2 cups all-purpose flour
2 tablespoons sugar
2 teaspoons baking powder
1/2 teaspoon baking soda
1/2 teaspoon salt
1/2 teaspoon ground cardamom or pure vanilla extract
1/4 cup (1/2 stick) unsalted butter, melted and cooled
Vegetable oil for cooking
Powdered sugar for sprinkling

In a bowl, beat the egg whites until stiff but not dry. Set aside.

In another bowl, combine the egg yolks, buttermilk, flour, sugar, baking powder, baking soda, salt, cardamom or vanilla, and melted butter and mix until smooth. Fold in the beaten egg whites.

Preheat an oven to 200° F.

Pour about 3/4 teaspoon oil into each round of an *aebleskiver* pan and heat over medium-high heat. Add a heaping tablespoon of the batter, or enough to fill each round about three-quarters full. When bubbly around the edges, turn each round upside down with chopsticks or a fork. Continue cooking, turning frequently, until the rounds are golden on all sides and done in the middle, about 5 minutes. Remove each cake as it is done and drain on paper towels. Keep warm in the oven until all rounds are cooked. Sprinkle with powdered sugar and serve warm.

Makes 6 to 8 servings.

Four-Grain Pancakes

The ingredients list would lead you to think these will be heavy, but they turn out light and scrumptious. Add seasonal berries or chopped bananas to the batter if you wish.

1 1/2 cups regular (not instant) rolled oats
3/4 cup buckwheat flour
3/4 cup whole wheat flour
3/4 cup polenta or coarse yellow cornmeal
4 teaspoons baking powder
1 1/2 teaspoons baking soda
4 1/2 cups buttermilk
1/4 cup pure maple syrup
2 eggs, or 4 egg whites, at room temperature
1/3 cup canola or other high-quality vegetable oil

In a bowl, combine the oats, buckwheat flour, whole wheat flour, polenta or cornmeal, baking powder, and baking soda and stir to blend well. Set aside.

In another bowl, combine the buttermilk, syrup, eggs, and oil, and blend well. Add the flour mixture and stir until the ingredients are just blended. Set aside to soften the grains before baking, about 15 minutes.

Meanwhile, heat a nonstick griddle or large, heavy skillet over medium-high heat, then lightly brush with melted butter or oil or spray with oil.

Pour the batter, about 1/4 cup for each pancake, onto the cooking surface. Cook until the tops are bubbly, then turn and cook until the bottoms are browned. Serve hot with your favorite toppings.

Makes 6 to 8 servings.

Spoon the batter, about a heaping tablespoon for each cake, onto the cooking surface. Cook, turning once, until crisp and golden on both sides. Serve hot.

Makes 4 servings.

Blueberry Corn Pancakes

These are my very favorite pancakes, especially with warm maple syrup. The golden color and crunchy texture of the corn are counterpointed by dark and juicy blueberries. When fresh berries are not available, unsweetened frozen ones work well.

1¹/2 cups yellow cornmeal
¹/2 cup all-purpose flour
1 teaspoon baking powder
¹/2 teaspoon baking soda
¹/2 teaspoon salt
2 cups buttermilk
2 tablespoons pure maple syrup or honey
2 tablespoons canola or other high-quality vegetable oil
1 egg, at room temperature
About 1¹/2 cups fresh blueberries

In a bowl, combine the cornmeal, flour, baking powder, baking soda, and salt and stir to blend well. Set aside.

In another bowl, combine the buttermilk, syrup or honey, oil, and egg, and blend well. Add the cornmeal mixture and stir until the indredients are just blended. Set aside for 10 minutes to soften the cornmeal.

Meanwhile, heat a nonstick griddle or large, heavy skillet over medium-high heat, then lightly brush with melted butter or oil or spray with oil.

Pour the batter, about ¹/4 cup for each pancake, onto the cooking surface. Scatter the berries over the batter and cook until the tops are bubbly, then turn and cook until the bottoms are browned. Wipe the pan with paper toweling to remove blueberry stains between batches. Serve hot.

Makes 4 servings.

Johnnycakes

Use plenty of butter or oil on the griddle in order for these traditional New England cakes to form crunchy crusts in contrast with their soft interiors. Serve with warm maple syrup.

1 cup white flint or other stone-ground cornmeal
¹/2 teaspoon salt
³/4 cup boiling water
2 tablespoons unsalted butter, melted
2 teaspoons sugar
¹/4 cup light cream or half and half

In a bowl, combine the cornmeal and salt, then gradually add the boiling water, stirring constantly to prevent lumps. Stir in the melted butter, sugar, and cream.

Meanwhile, heat a griddle or large, heavy skillet over medium-high heat, then generously brush with melted butter or oil or spray with oil.

Puffed Oven-Baked Pancakes

Known by such picturesque names as "Dutch Babies" and "Bismarks," these showy German classics are among my favorite breakfast treats for entertaining. The basic recipe is for individual pancakes. For larger groups, multiply all ingredients as you increase the pan size. I often bake awe-inspiring giant versions in a shallow paella pan that holds a dozen times the batter recipe.

Choose an ovenproof skillet, pie pan, or other shallow baking dish that will hold the desired number of servings. For a single serving, shown here, use a 4-inch diameter container. For a 2-egg individual pancake, shown on the cover, use a 6-inch pan. For 4 to 6 eggs, use a 9- to 10-inch pan; for 6 to 8 eggs, use a 12-inch pan; for 10 to 12 eggs, use a 14- to 16-inch pan. As a general rule, larger pans that spread the batter thinner yield a drier and puffier pancake, while a thicker layer of batter in smaller pans produces a more custardy pancake and may take a bit longer to cook completely.

The classic topping is a generous sprinkling of powdered sugar and a squeeze of lemon or lime. Other possibilities include fresh berries, sliced seasonal fruit, or any of the toppings suggested on page 36. No matter which toppings you choose, present them at the table for adding according to taste. Be sure to have the whole breakfast on the table and everyone seated before bringing the showy pancake directly from the oven.

FOR EACH SERVING:
1 tablespoon unsalted butter
1 egg
¹/₄ cup milk (not nonfat)
¹/₄ cup all-purpose flour
¹/₈ teaspoon salt

Preheat an oven to 475° F.

Select a baking pan or dish (see recipe introduction). Add the butter (you'll need enough to generously coat the bottom of the baking

container) and heat in the oven until the butter is melted and the container is hot; watch carefully to avoid burning the butter.

Meanwhile, calculate the number of servings and multiply the ingredients accordingly. In a blender, combine the egg(s), milk, flour, and salt and blend until smooth. Pour the batter into the heated baking pan or dish and return the pan to the oven. Cook until the pancake is well puffed and golden, about 12 minutes, or longer for larger pancakes or those with a thicker layer of batter. Serve at once. When you make larger pancakes, cut them into wedges at the table, or spread with selected topping, roll up jelly-roll fashion, and cut crosswise into slices at the table.

Skillet Cake with Sautéed Apples

Former cooking teacher Babs Lonon introduced this recipe into my entertaining repertoire.

1/2 cup (1 stick) unsalted butter
4 or 5 Golden Delicious or other firm, flavorful apples, cored and thinly sliced
3/4 cup packed brown sugar
1 cup all-purpose flour
1 teaspoon baking powder
1/2 teaspoon baking soda
1/4 teaspoon salt
3 eggs, separated
1 cup buttermilk
1/2 pint (1 cup) sour cream or plain yogurt

In a sauté pan or skillet, melt 6 tablespoons of the butter over medium heat. Add the apples and sauté until they are tender but still hold their shape, about 10 minutes, covering for the last few minutes. When almost done, stir in the brown sugar. Cover, set aside, and keep warm.

In a bowl, combine the flour, baking powder, baking soda, and salt and stir to blend well. Set aside.

In another bowl, beat the egg whites until stiff but not dry. Set aside.

In another bowl, combine the egg yolks and buttermilk and beat until smooth. Add the flour mixture and stir until just moistened. Add the egg whites and gently fold until incorporated.

Preheat a broiler.

In a 10-inch skillet, melt the remaining 2 tablespoons butter over medium heat. Add the batter and cook until set, 3 to 5 minutes. Place the skillet about 4 inches under the preheated broiler and continue cooking until the top is lightly browned. Test with a wooden skewer; if not dry, place over low heat and cook until done.

Turn the cake onto a very large serving platter. Surround the cake with the sautéed apples and top with sour cream or yogurt. Cut into wedges to serve.

Makes 4 servings.

Monkey Bread

This is a special delight to children of all ages. Use your favorite recipe for whole wheat bread, or purchase a good brand of frozen honey-wheat bread dough. For the ultimate sensation, use the dough for Brioche (page 32) or Croissants (page 34). If using frozen dough, thaw it overnight in the refrigerator; it will be ready to use in the morning.

¾ **cup sugar**
¾ **cup packed light brown sugar**
2 teaspoons ground cinnamon
Dough for 3 loaves honey-sweetened whole wheat bread, risen,
  or 3 loaves high-quality frozen commercial honey-wheat
  bread dough, thawed
About ½ cup (1 stick) unsalted butter, melted

Heavily grease a 10-inch tube cake pan and set aside.

In a shallow bowl, combine the sugar, brown sugar, and cinnamon and mix well.

Lightly dust your hands with flour and tear off pieces of risen dough about 1½ inches in diameter. Roll each piece into a round ball. Dip a dough ball into the melted butter, then roll in the cinnamon sugar until completely coated, and place in the pan. Continue to coat the balls and place in the pan about ½ inch apart, layering until the dough is used or the pan is about three-quarters full. Cover with a kitchen towel and let stand in a warm place until the dough rises to the top of the pan, about 30 minutes.

Preheat an oven to 350° F.

Bake until a wooden skewer inserted in the center of the bread comes out clean, about 1 hour, covering loosely with foil if the top begins to get too brown. Remove from the oven and let cool for 5 to 10 minutes, then unmold and serve warm. To eat, pull the loaf apart.

Makes 1 loaf, enough for 6 to 10 servings.

VARIATION: Sprinkle raisins and/or chopped nuts between the layers and on top of the dough.

Toast Toppings

Turn routine morning toast into something special by topping it with one of the following combinations before grilling in a toaster oven until the topping is bubbly. Or lightly brown one side of the bread under a broiler, then turn and add topping to the other side and heat until the topping is bubbly.

Spread top side with unsalted butter and generously sprinkle with ground cinnamon and sugar to taste.

Spread top side with unsalted butter or peanut butter, then cover with sliced bananas and drizzle with honey.

Spread top side lightly with butter, then cover with sliced or shredded cheese. Sprinkle with ground cayenne or other hot chile to taste.

Spread top side with unsalted butter, then cover with finely chopped nuts and drizzle with honey.

Sticky Buns

Those gooey glazed sticky buns and cinnamon rolls that are the rage at bakeries coast to coast are easy to make at home.

SWEET YEAST DOUGH
1/4 cup warm water (110° to 115° F)
1/2 cup sugar
2 packages (1/4 ounce *each*) quick-rising active dry yeast
3 eggs, at room temperature
1 1/2 teaspoons salt
1 cup milk (not nonfat)
1/2 cup (1 stick) unsalted butter, melted and cooled
5 3/4 cups all-purpose flour

CURRANT-PECAN FILLING
1 1/2 cups packed brown sugar
1/2 cup (1 stick) unsalted butter, softened
1 1/2 tablespoons ground cinnamon
1/2 cup dried currants
3/4 cup finely chopped pecans

STICKY PECAN GLAZE
1 cup (2 sticks) unsalted butter, softened
1 3/4 cups packed brown sugar
1/4 cup light corn syrup
3/4 cup small pecan halves or coarsely chopped pecans

To make the Sweet Yeast Dough, in a small bowl, combine the warm water and 1 tablespoon of the sugar, sprinkle with the yeast, stir to dissolve, and set aside until soft and foamy, about 5 minutes. (Discard the mixture and start over with fresh packages of yeast if bubbles have not formed within 5 minutes.)

In the bowl of a stand mixer fitted with a flat beater, combine the remaining 7 tablespoons sugar, the eggs, salt, milk, butter, and the foamy yeast mixture and mix at the lowest speed until smooth. With the mixer running at low speed, add the flour, 1/2 cup at a time, until well incorporated, stopping to scrape down the bowl and beater as necessary. Exchange the beater for a dough hook. Knead at medium speed until the dough is smooth, elastic, and no longer sticky, about

3 minutes. Gather the dough into a ball, transfer to a lightly buttered bowl, turn the dough to coat all sides with butter, cover the bowl tightly with plastic wrap, and let rise in a warm place until doubled in bulk, about 1 hour.

Meanwhile, to make the Currant-Pecan Filling, in a bowl, combine all of the filling ingredients, mix well, and set aside.

To make the Sticky Pecan Glaze, in another bowl, combine the butter, brown sugar, and corn syrup and beat until well mixed. Butter the bottoms of two 9-inch round cake pans and spread the mixture evenly in the pans. Sprinkle with the pecans and set aside.

Punch the risen dough down, turn it out onto a lightly floured surface, and roll it out into a 14-by-24-inch rectangle. Sprinkle the reserved filling over the dough, gently pressing the mixture into the dough with your fingers. Beginning with the short end, roll the dough up like a jelly roll. Slice crosswise into 1-inch-wide pieces to make a total of 14 slices. Arrange 7 slices on top of the glaze in each pan. Cover with a kitchen towel and let stand in a warm place until puffy and almost doubled in bulk, about 1 hour.

Preheat an oven to 375° F.

Bake the buns until golden brown on top, about 20 minutes. Remove from the oven, immediately cover each pan with an inverted serving platter, quickly invert, and lift off the pans; the glaze will dribble down the sides. Pull apart and serve warm.

Makes 14 buns.

VARIATIONS: For a heartier bun, substitute 2 cups whole wheat flour for 2 cups of the all-purpose flour.

For cinnamon rolls, omit the Sticky Pecan Glaze. Bake in buttered pans, then turn out and brush tops with a mixture of 3/4 cup powdered sugar, 1 tablespoon warm water, and 1 tablespoon freshly squeezed lemon juice.

Filled Raised Coffee Cake

This big, moist coffee cake serves a crowd.

Sweet Yeast Dough (page 46)
1 teaspoon powdered saffron (optional)
2 cups golden raisins, soaked in hot water until plumped, then
    drained
2 cups drained canned juice-packed crushed pineapple
3 tablespoons grated or minced fresh orange zest
2 tablespoons grated or minced fresh lemon zest
2¹/₂ cups chopped pecans
1 cup packed light brown sugar
2 tablespoons ground cinnamon
1 cup (2 sticks) unsalted butter, softened

Make the Sweet Yeast Dough as directed, adding the saffron
(if using) along with the yeast. Then follow all steps through the
first rising.

Meanwhile, to make the filling, in a bowl, combine the raisins,
pineapple, and orange and lemon zests, mix well, and set aside.

In a small bowl, combine the nuts, brown sugar, and cinnamon and
mix well. Set aside.

Punch the risen dough down and turn it out onto a lightly floured
surface. Divide the dough into 2 equal pieces, then roll out each piece
to fit into a 9-by-13-inch baking pan. Grease the pan and place one
sheet of dough in the bottom. Spread with half of the softened butter,
then sprinkle with half of the raisin mixture and half of the nut
mixture. Cover with the second sheet of rolled dough, then spread
with the remaining butter and top with the remaining raisin mixture
and nut mixture. Cover with a kitchen towel and let rise in a warm
place until the dough is puffy and doubled in bulk, about 1 hour.

Preheat an oven to 375° F.

Line a larger rimmed baking sheet or pan with aluminum foil and
place on an oven rack below the coffee cake pan to catch any drips.
Bake the cake until golden brown and a wooden skewer inserted in
the center comes out clean, 30 to 40 minutes, covering loosely with
foil if the top begins to get too brown. Remove from the oven and
cool slightly before serving. To serve, cut into squares.

Makes 16 servings.

Sour Cream Breakfast Cake with Pecan and Cinnamon Filling

The aroma from the oven as this easy cake bakes will arouse even the laziest person in the house. It can also be made a day or two ahead, covered after cooling, and stored at room temperature.

PECAN AND CINNAMON FILLING
1¹/₂ cups chopped lightly toasted pecans
³/₄ cup packed brown sugar
1 tablespoon ground cinnamon

SOUR CREAM CAKE
3 cups all-purpose flour
1 tablespoon baking powder
1 teaspoon baking soda
¹/₂ teaspoon salt
1 cup (2 sticks) unsalted butter, at room temperature
1¹/₂ cups sugar
3 eggs, at room temperature, lightly beaten
1 tablespoon grated or minced fresh lemon zest
1 teaspoon pure vanilla extract
1¹/₂ cups sour cream (not nonfat), at room temperature
Powdered sugar for dusting

To make the Pecan and Cinnamon Filling, in a bowl, combine the pecans, brown sugar, and cinnamon and stir to mix well. Set aside.

Preheat an oven to 350° F. Grease and flour a 10-inch fluted tube pan and set aside.

To make the Sour Cream Cake, place the flour, baking powder, baking soda, and salt together into a sifter or fine sieve and sift onto a sheet of waxed paper or into a bowl. Set aside.

In the bowl of a standing mixer fitted with a flat beater, or in a bowl using a hand mixer, beat the butter until soft and creamy, about 45 seconds. With the mixer still running, slowly add the sugar, then stop the mixer and scrape the mixture that clings to the sides of the

bowl into the center. Continue beating until very light and fluffy, about 5 minutes. Slowly pour in the eggs and beat until smooth, about 2 minutes. Stir in the lemon zest and vanilla.

Using the mixer on low speed or a rubber spatula, fold in about half of the flour mixture, then the sour cream, and finally the remaining flour mixture.

Spoon about half of the batter into the prepared pan. Sprinkle the reserved filling evenly down the center of the batter, preventing the filling from touching the sides of the pan. Cover with the remaining batter. Bake until a wooden skewer inserted in the thickest part comes out clean, 45 to 55 minutes. Remove the pan to a wire rack to cool for about 10 minutes, then turn the cake out onto the rack to cool completely. Place on a serving plate and dust with powdered sugar.

Makes a 10-inch cake, enough for 12 servings.

Upside-Down Breakfast Cake

The elegant look of this cake belies the quick and easy technique. If you use blueberries or blackberries, add lemon juice and zest in the batter; when you choose cranberries, use the orange juice and zest. Serve with cream for pouring over the cake, or unsweetened whipped cream, plain yogurt, or a custard sauce.

1/2 cup (1 stick) plus 2 tablespoons unsalted butter,
    at room temperature
1 cup packed light brown sugar
2 1/2 cups fresh blueberries, blackberries, or cranberries
1 1/2 cups all-purpose flour
2 1/2 teaspoons baking powder
1/2 teaspoon salt
3/4 cup sugar
2 eggs, at room temperature, lightly beaten
1/4 cup freshly squeezed lemon juice, or 1/2 cup freshly squeezed
    orange juice
1 tablespoon grated or minced fresh lemon zest, or 2 tablespoons
    grated or minced fresh orange zest
1/2 teaspoon pure vanilla extract
1/3 cup milk (not nonfat), at room temperature

Preheat an oven to 350° F. Lightly butter a 9-inch round cake pan and set aside.

In a bowl, combine 2 tablespoons of the butter and the brown sugar and mix well. Spread the mixture evenly in the bottom of the prepared pan. Spread the berries evenly over the mixture and set aside.

Place the flour, baking powder, and salt together into a sifter or fine sieve and sift onto a sheet of waxed paper or into a bowl. Set aside.

In the bowl of a standing mixer fitted with a flat beater, or in a bowl using a hand mixer, beat the remaining 1/2 cup butter at medium speed until soft and creamy, about 45 seconds. With the mixer still running, slowly add the sugar, then stop the mixer and scrape the mixture that clings to the sides of the bowl into the center. Continue beating until very light and fluffy, about 5 minutes. Slowly pour in the eggs and beat until smooth, about 2 minutes. Stir in the lemon or orange juice and zest and vanilla.

Using the mixer on low speed or a rubber spatula, fold in about half of the flour mixture, then the milk, and finally the remaining flour mixture.

Spoon the batter over the berries. Bake until the top is golden and a wooden skewer inserted in the center comes out clean, 50 to 55 minutes. Remove from the oven, run a knife around the inside edge of the pan, cover the cake with a serving plate, and invert the cake onto the plate, fruit side up. Cool slightly before serving warm.

Makes a 9-inch cake, enough for 8 to 12 servings.

Creamy Rice Pudding Brûlée

This cross between rice pudding and *crème brûlée* makes a memorable ending to a holiday or weekend breakfast.

3/4 cup long-grain white rice
6 egg yolks, at room temperature
1/4 cup sugar
2 1/4 cups heavy (whipping) cream, light cream, or half and half, heated almost to boiling
Brown sugar for sprinkling

In a saucepan, combine the rice and 1 1/2 cups water, place over high heat, and bring to a boil, then cover tightly, reduce the heat to very low, and simmer until the rice is tender and the water is absorbed, about 15 minutes. Set aside to cool.

Preheat an oven to 250° F. Butter a 9-inch pie plate or other shallow baking dish, place it in a larger baking pan, and set aside.

In a bowl, beat the egg yolks and sugar with a wire whisk or hand mixer until light and fluffy, then gradually add the hot cream and beat until smooth. Add the rice and stir to blend thoroughly. Pour the mixture into the reserved pie pan or baking dish. Transfer to the oven and pour enough hot (not boiling) water into the larger pan to reach about halfway up the sides of the baking dish. Bake until the custard is set and a knife inserted in the center comes out clean, about 1 hour.

Remove from the oven and let cool to room temperature, then refrigerate until thoroughly chilled, up to overnight.

One or two hours before serving, preheat a broiler.

Sprinkle the top of the custard with a thin even layer of brown sugar. Using a mister, lightly spray the sugar with a little water. Place under the preheated broiler until the sugar melts and bubbles, about 1 minute. Chill at least 20 minutes or up to 2 hours before serving. Cut into wedges.

Makes 8 servings.

Indian Pudding

One of America's oldest desserts adds a new dimension to the breakfast menu.

1/2 cup yellow cornmeal
1/2 cup molasses
4 cups milk (not nonfat), heated almost to boiling
2 tablespoons unsalted butter, melted
1 teaspoon ground cinnamon
1 teaspoon ground ginger
1/2 teaspoon ground allspice
1/2 teaspoon salt
2 eggs, at room temperature
Heavy (whipping) cream, light cream, or half and half for serving

Preheat an oven to 350° F. Generously butter a 1 1/2-quart baking dish, place it in a larger baking pan, and set aside.

Pour 2 inches of water into the bottom part of a double boiler and bring to a simmer over medium-high heat, then adjust the heat to maintain a simmer.

In the top part of the double boiler, combine the cornmeal and the molasses, then whisk in the hot milk until well blended and smooth. Place over the simmering water and cook, stirring almost constantly, until thick and smooth, about 15 minutes. Remove from the simmering water and stir in the butter, spices, and salt.

In a small bowl, beat the eggs, then stir in about 1/4 cup of the hot pudding. Transfer to the pudding and stir until well blended.

Pour the mixture into the prepared baking dish. Transfer to the oven and pour enough hot (not boiling) water into the larger pan to reach about halfway up the sides of the baking dish. Bake, stirring occasionally, until set, about 2 hours.

Serve warm. Pass cream for drizzling over the top.

Makes 6 servings.

Breakfast Bread Pudding

It may sound decadent for breakfast, but a warm bread pudding can be a comforting way to begin a special wintry day. The ingredients provide the same nutrition—eggs, dairy products, carbohydrates, fruit—as French toast or many other breakfast favorites.

8 ounces stale French bread
2 eggs
3/4 cup sugar
3 cups milk (not nonfat)
1 cup heavy (whipping) cream, light cream, or half-and-half
1/2 cup (1 stick) unsalted butter, melted
1 tablespoon pure vanilla extract
3/4 cup dried currants or raisins
1 teaspoon freshly grated nutmeg
Powdered sugar for dusting
Lemon Sauce or Warm Berry Sauce (see adjacent recipes)

Cut the bread into slices about 1/2 inch thick. If crusts are tough, trim off and discard. Place the slices in a large bowl.

In another bowl, combine the eggs, sugar, milk, cream, melted butter, vanilla, currants, and nutmeg and whisk to blend well. Pour the mixture over the bread slices and let stand, turning the bread as necessary, until the bread is soft and saturated, about 30 minutes.

Lightly butter a 4-quart baking dish and arrange the bread slices in it. Pour any unabsorbed custard mixture over the bread. (At this point, the pudding can be covered and refrigerated for up to overnight.)

Preheat an oven to 350° F.

Bake, uncovered, until the custard is set and top is lightly browned, about 45 minutes.

Meanwhile, prepare one of the sauces and keep warm.

To serve, dust the top of the pudding with powdered sugar. Pass the warm sauce at the table.

Makes 8 servings.

Lemon Sauce

This is my favorite topping for Breakfast Bread Pudding. It's also good in place of syrup on other morning treats. It may be made ahead, refrigerated, and gently reheated before serving.

1 cup sugar
Pinch of salt
1 1/2 tablespoons cornstarch
1 cup boiling water
3 tablespoons unsalted butter
1/4 cup freshly squeezed lemon juice
1 tablespoon minced or grated fresh lemon zest
1 drop yellow food coloring (optional)

In a saucepan, combine the sugar, salt, and cornstarch. Slowly stir in the boiling water, blending well. Place over low heat and cook, stirring constantly, until the sauce is clear and thickened, about 5 minutes.

Remove from the heat. Add the butter, lemon juice and zest, and food coloring (if using) and stir until the butter melts. Serve warm.

Makes about 1 1/2 cups.

Warm Berry Sauce

In addition to serving with the adjacent bread pudding, this sweet and tangy sauce is delicious over pancakes, waffles, or French toast.

2 cups fresh or frozen raspberries
2 cups fresh or frozen strawberries
1/3 cup sugar
1/3 cup freshly squeezed orange juice
3 tablespoons freshly squeezed lemon juice

In a saucepan, combine all of the ingredients and place over medium heat. Cook, stirring constantly, until the fruit begins to break up, about 5 minutes. Transfer to a food processor or blender and puree. Reheat just before serving.

Makes about 2 cups.

French Toast

The French call it *pain perdu*, or "lost bread," because it's made with leftover bread that would otherwise be discarded—or perhaps because it's hidden in batter. In addition to classic French bread, try making this with whole wheat cinnamon bread or other hearty grain breads. Top with honey, syrup, preserves, or other favorite toppings.

4 eggs
1 cup milk (not nonfat)
1 tablespoon sugar, honey, or pure maple syrup
¼ teaspoon salt
1 teaspoon ground cinnamon
1 teaspoon freshly grated nutmeg
1 tablespoon minced fresh tarragon, or 1 teaspoon crumbled dried
    tarragon (optional)
½ teaspoon pure vanilla extract
8 1½-inch-thick slices day-old French-style bread, sweet or
    sourdough
About ½ cup (1 stick) unsalted butter
Powdered sugar for dusting

In a large bowl, combine the eggs, milk, sugar or other sweetener, salt, cinnamon, nutmeg, tarragon (if using), and vanilla and beat until well mixed. Place the bread slices into the mixture, turning to thoroughly coat both sides. Let stand, turning occasionally, until most of the liquid is absorbed.

In a skillet, heat 2 tablespoons of the butter over medium-low heat until foamy. Add as many of the bread slices that will fit without crowding the pan and cook until golden brown on each side, turning once and adding additional butter as needed. Cook the remaining bread in the same way. Dust with powdered sugar and serve hot.

Makes 4 servings.

Fried Polenta

Use leftovers of this Italian treat from dinner, or make it ahead just to have on hand for breakfast. Drizzle with warmed honey or maple syrup at the table.

1 tablespoon salt
2 cups polenta or coarsely ground yellow cornmeal
½ cup (1 stick) unsalted butter
Honey or pure maple syrup, warmed

In a deep saucepan, bring 6 cups water to a boil over high heat. Add the salt and reduce the heat to maintain a simmer. While stirring continuously with a long-handled wooden spoon, add the polenta in a slow, steady stream. Cook, stirring frequently, until the polenta is thick enough for the spoon to stand upright, about 20 minutes. Cut 4 tablespoons (½ stick) of the butter into small pieces, add to the polenta, and stir until the butter melts. Pour into a lightly greased 9-by-5-inch loaf pan, pressing it evenly into the corners. Cover with plastic wrap and refrigerate overnight or for up to 3 days.

To remove the polenta loaf, briefly dip the pan into hot water and slide a blunt knife blade around the edges. Invert the loaf onto a flat surface and remove the pan. Slice as you would bread.

Preheat an oven to 200° F.

In a large skillet, melt the remaining butter, about 2 tablespoons at a time as needed, over medium-high heat. Add a few polenta slices at a time and fry until golden brown on one side, about 8 to 10 minutes. Turn and brown the other sides, about 8 to 10 minutes more. Transfer to an ovenproof dish and keep warm in the oven until all the slices are cooked, using the remaining butter as needed. Serve warm.

Makes 6 servings.

New Orleans Raised Rice Cakes
(Calas)

In old New Orleans, black women roamed the French Quarter streets calling *"Belle cala! Tout chaud!"* ("Lovely rice! Piping hot!") The word *cala* is derived from an African word for rice. Cook the mushy rice the night before and combine it with yeast to rise overnight.

Pass a pitcher of Louisiana cane syrup or a bowl of strawberry jam at the table.

¹/₂ cup long-grain white rice
1 teaspoon salt
1 package (¹/₄ ounce) active dry yeast
¹/₂ cup warm water (110° to 115° F)
¹/₄ cup sugar
1 teaspoon ground cinnamon
1 teaspoon freshly grated nutmeg
1¹/₄ cups all-purpose flour
3 eggs, well beaten
Peanut or other high-quality vegetable oil for frying
Powdered sugar for dusting
Dark cane syrup or strawberry jam for serving

In a heavy saucepan, combine the rice, 1¹/₂ cups water, and salt and bring to a boil over high heat. Cover the pan, reduce the heat to very low, and simmer until the rice is very soft, about 25 minutes. Drain off any excess water and transfer the rice to a large bowl. Mash the rice with a wooden spoon and let cool to room temperature.

In a small bowl, sprinkle the yeast over the warm water, stir, and set aside until soft and foamy, about 5 minutes. (Discard the mixture and start over with a fresh package of yeast if bubbles have not formed within 5 minutes.)

Add the foamy yeast to the rice, stirring to thoroughly combine. Cover the bowl with plastic wrap and set in a warm place to rise overnight.

The next morning, add the sugar, cinnamon, nutmeg, flour, and eggs to the rice and beat well. Cover with a kitchen towel and set in a warm place to rise for about 30 minutes.

In a deep fryer or saucepan, pour in oil to a depth of 3 inches and heat to 375° F. Place a wire rack on a baking sheet and position alongside the fryer or stove top. Preheat an oven to 200° F.

Moisten your hands with water, then take about 1 tablespoon of the dough and roll it into a ball. Carefully add it to the hot oil, then repeat to add a few more; avoid crowding the pan. Cook, turning frequently with tongs or a slotted utensil, until golden brown and crusty. Transfer to the rack to drain well, then place the rack in the oven to keep warm. Fry the remaining dough in the same manner, allowing the oil to return to 375° F between batches.

Dust the *calas* with powdered sugar and serve hot.

Makes 6 servings.

French Doughnut Squares
(Beignets)

During my years in New Orleans, my favorite breakfast—no matter what time of day or night—was a steaming mug of *café au lait* and a plate of powdered-sugar-dusted *beignets* in the French Market. This is as close as I can come to the originals served at Café du Monde and the old Morning Call.

If you can't use all the dough at one time, store it unrolled in the refrigerator for up to five days, breaking off and rolling only what you need at a time.

Serve with *café au lait* or strong coffee (see page 8).

3/4 cup warm water (110° to 115° F)
1/2 package (1/8 ounce) quick-rising active dry yeast
1/4 cup sugar
1/2 teaspoon salt
1/2 cup canned evaporated milk (not nonfat)
1 egg, lightly beaten
2 tablespoons solid vegetable shortening
3 1/2 cups all-purpose flour
Pure lard or peanut or other high-quality vegetable oil for frying
Powdered sugar for dusting

In a small bowl, combine the warm water and 1 tablespoon of the sugar, sprinkle with the yeast, stir to dissolve, and set aside until soft and foamy, about 5 minutes. (Discard the mixture and start over with a fresh package of yeast if bubbles have not formed within 5 minutes.)

In the bowl of a stand mixer fitted with a flat beater, combine the remaining 3 tablespoons sugar, the salt, evaporated milk, egg, shortening, and the foamy yeast mixture and mix at the lowest speed until smooth. With the mixer still running, add the flour, 1/2 cup at a time, stopping to scrape down the bowl and beater as necessary, until well blended. Transfer the dough to a lightly greased bowl, cover the bowl tightly with plastic wrap, and set aside in a warm place to relax the gluten for about 30 minutes, then refrigerate for at least 4 hours or up to overnight.

In a deep fryer or saucepan, melt lard or pour in oil to a depth of 3 inches and heat to 360° F. Place a wire rack on a baking sheet and position alongside the fryer or stove top. Preheat an oven to 200° F.

Gather the chilled dough into a ball and pat or roll it out on a lightly floured surface to a thickness of about 1/4 inch. Using a sharp knife, cut the dough into 2-by-3-inch rectangles. Carefully add a few to the hot oil; avoid crowding the pan. Cook, turning frequently with tongs or a slotted utensil, until golden brown on all sides. Transfer to the rack to drain well, then place the rack in the oven to keep warm. Fry the remaining dough in the same manner, allowing the oil to return to 360° F between batches.

Sprinkle generously with powdered sugar and serve hot.

Makes about 36 *beignets.*

DAIRY & EGGS

Breakfast Custard

Ever since I learned to make silken custard bathed in amber-hued caramel from watching Julia Child on television many years ago, I've loved this soothing sweet at any time of the day. If you enjoy the flavor of maple as much as I do, try substituting granulated maple sugar for a change of pace.

Serve warm or cold, plain or with seasonal fruit.

1¹/₂ cups sugar
2¹/₂ cups whole milk or canned evaporated milk
1 vanilla bean, split, or 1 teaspoon pure vanilla extract
3 whole eggs
5 egg yolks
Fresh berries and sliced fruits for garnish (optional)

In a heavy saucepan, combine 1 cup of the sugar with ¹/₄ cup water and stir well. Place over medium heat, cover, and heat for about 4 minutes. Remove the cover and continue to cook, swirling the pan, until the syrup turns amber, about 8 minutes longer. If sugar crystals begin to form around the sides of the pan just above the bubbling syrup, brush them away with a wet brush. Immediately remove from the heat and carefully pour the hot syrup into a 2-quart baking dish or pan, turning the container in all directions to coat the bottom and sides with the caramel until the syrup is hard. Place the dish in a larger baking pan and set aside.

In another saucepan, combine the milk and vanilla bean, place over medium heat, and bring almost to a boil. (If you are using vanilla extract, do not add it yet.) Remove from the heat, cover, and set aside.

Preheat an oven to 350° F.

In a mixing bowl, combine the eggs and egg yolks and beat lightly with a fork until as smooth as possible; avoid overbeating at any point to prevent too many air bubbles from forming. Stir in the remaining ¹/₂ cup sugar and the warm milk. Stir in the vanilla extract if you did not use the bean. Strain the mixture through a fine sieve into the caramel-coated dish. Cover the top of the custard dish with aluminum foil or parchment paper. Transfer in the larger pan to the lower rack of the oven and pour enough hot (not boiling) water into the larger pan to come halfway up the sides of the custard dish.

Bake until a knife inserted near the edge of the custard comes out barely clean, about 50 minutes; the center should still wobble slightly when the dish is shaken. Regulate the oven temperature during baking to maintain water at the almost simmering stage; do not allow to boil. Immediately remove from the hot water to a countertop, remove the foil or paper, and let cool slightly.

To serve warm, run a thin knife blade around the inside of the baking dish to loosen the custard. Cover with an inverted serving plate and quickly invert the custard. Lift off the baking dish; caramel syrup will run down onto the serving dish to surround the custard. Surround with fresh fruit (if using).

To serve cold, let cool to room temperature, then cover tightly and refrigerate until well chilled, at least 3 hours or up to overnight. Just before serving, immerse the bottom of the dish in a pan of hot water for about 30 seconds, then loosen custard, unmold, and garnish as above.

Makes 6 to 8 servings.

Cheese Blintzes

These Jewish crêpes can be filled and refrigerated up to 24 hours ahead. Brown them in butter just before serving with sour cream and your favorite preserves.

CHEESE FILLING
3 ounces cream cheese, at room temperature
1 cup fresh farmer's or pot cheese or small-curd cottage cheese (about 1/2 pound)
3 tablespoons sugar
1 egg yolk
3/4 teaspoon pure vanilla extract
1 teaspoon grated or minced fresh lemon zest

CRÊPE BATTER
1 cup sifted all-purpose flour
1/4 teaspoon salt
1 cup milk (not nonfat)
2 eggs

About 1/2 cup (1 stick) unsalted butter for cooking
Sour cream or crème fraîche for serving
Fruit preserves for serving

To make the Cheese Filling, in a bowl, combine the cheeses, sugar, egg yolk, vanilla, and lemon zest. Mix with a wire whisk or fork until light and fluffy, and set aside.

To make the Crêpe Batter, in a blender, combine the flour, salt, milk, and eggs and blend until smooth.

Heat an 8-inch nonstick skillet over medium-high heat. Add enough butter to coat the bottom of the pan. When the butter melts, ladle or pour in about 2 tablespoons of the batter and tilt the pan to coat the bottom evenly with a thin coating of batter. Cook the crêpe on one side only, just until it begins to curl away from the sides of the pan, 1 to 2 minutes. Slide the crêpe onto a plate and repeat until all the batter is used, adding butter to the pan as needed and stacking crêpes as they are cooked. You should have about 12 crêpes.

To assemble the blintzes, place about 2 tablespoons of the cheese filling on the center of the uncooked side of each crêpe. Fold in the sides to form small square packets.

In a large skillet, melt 2 to 3 tablespoons of the remaining butter over medium-high heat. Place 3 to 4 blintzes in the pan, seam side down, and cook, turning once, until golden brown on both sides, about 2 to 3 minutes total cooking time. Repeat with the remaining blintzes, adding more butter as needed. Serve the blintzes at once, topped with sour cream or crème fraîche and your favorite preserves.

Makes 12 blintzes, enough for 4 servings.

Cheese Soufflé

Use any one of your favorite cheeses or a compatible combination for a soufflé. Add favorite fresh or dried herbs, sautéed minced mushrooms, or finely crumbled cooked bacon if desired.

Be sure everyone is seated at the table before the soufflé is done.

1/4 cup (1/2 stick) unsalted butter
1/4 cup all-purpose flour
1/2 teaspoon salt
1/4 teaspoon freshly grated nutmeg
Freshly ground black pepper
1 1/2 cups milk (not nonfat)
1 1/2 cups freshly shredded Gruyère or other good-melting cheese (about 6 ounces)
6 eggs, separated
2 egg whites
1/2 teaspoon cream of tartar

(continued)

Preheat an oven to 350° F. Butter a 2-quart soufflé or other baking dish and set aside.

In a medium-sized saucepan, melt the butter over medium-high heat. Using a wire whisk, stir in the flour, salt, nutmeg, and pepper to taste, and whisk until smooth. Add the milk, whisking until smooth, and cook, stirring frequently, until thick and smooth, about 10 minutes. Add the cheese and stir until it melts and the mixture is smooth. Remove from the heat and beat in the egg yolks, one at a time.

In a large bowl, combine all of the egg whites and beat until frothy. Add the cream of tartar and continue beating until soft peaks form. Using a rubber spatula, fold about half of the whites into the cheese mixture. Gently fold in the remaining whites. Pour into the prepared soufflé dish.

Fold sheets of foil or baking parchment to form a collar around the top of the soufflé dish to prevent the soufflé from running over. Butter the inside of the collar and crimp ends to hold the collar in place. Bake until the soufflé is well browned and the top crust feels firm when gently tapped, 35 to 40 minutes. Do not open the door until the soufflé is almost done. Remove the collar and serve immediately.

Makes 6 servings.

Ricotta Cheese Torta

Flaky phyllo dough encases a slightly sweet cheese filling in this dish, which should be eaten with orange slices or peeled orange segments. In the original edition of this book, the flour was omitted from the filling ingredients list. Here is the correct version.

8 ounces cream cheese, softened
3 egg yolks
2 cups ricotta cheese, well drained
1/2 cup all-purpose flour
1/3 cup sugar

1/4 teaspoon salt
3 tablespoons grated or minced fresh orange zest
2 teaspoons pure vanilla extract
**10 sheets (about 1/2 pound) phyllo pastry,
    thawed (in the refrigerator) if frozen**
About 1/2 cup (1 stick) unsalted butter, melted and cooled
Powdered sugar for dusting

In a bowl, beat the cream cheese with a hand mixer until fluffy. Add the egg yolks and beat until smooth. Stir in the ricotta, flour, sugar, salt, orange zest, and vanilla until just combined.

Preheat an oven to 400° F.

Place 1 sheet of phyllo on a flat work surface. Keep the remaining dough covered with a lightly dampened towel to prevent it from drying out. With a wide pastry brush, lightly brush the sheet with cooled melted butter to completely cover. Top that phyllo sheet with a second sheet placed at a 45-degree angle to the first sheet and lightly brush it with butter. Repeat until all sheets are used and the sheets form a rough circle of dough. Spoon the cheese mixture onto the center of the top sheet to form a circle about 8 inches in diameter. Bring one side of the phyllo up and over to cover the cheese and brush the top of the dough with butter. Bring the remaining phyllo sides up and over the cheese, overlapping and buttering them as you go, until all sides of the phyllo have been folded over the cheese. Place the phyllo package, seam side down, on a baking sheet and brush the top with melted butter.

Bake until the phyllo is golden brown, about 15 minutes. Remove from the oven, dust lightly with powdered sugar, and serve immediately.

Makes 6 servings.

Soft-Cooked Eggs

I first came to enjoy soft-cooked eggs in Holland, where they star at almost every breakfast, along with sliced cold cuts, assorted cheeses, and breads.

Eggs, at room temperature

In a saucepan, combine the eggs with just enough water to cover. Remove the eggs and bring the water just to a simmer over medium heat. Carefully lower the eggs into the water. Adjust the heat to maintain a simmer and cook, uncovered, until the eggs are done to your taste, 3 to 5 minutes. Drain, and serve the eggs in egg cups. Crack the tops gently with a knife and peel away about 1/2 inch of the shell; eat with a spoon. Alternatively, crack and peel the eggs and serve in small bowls.

Each cooked egg makes 1 serving.

VARIATIONS: Top the cracked eggs with dollops of caviar, sour cream and minced chives, or sautéed crab or tiny shrimp.

Hard-Cooked Eggs

Don't call them "boiled" eggs, because boiling ruins eggs by turning the insides rubbery and cracking the shells, which then leak and create watery eggs.

Eggs, at room temperature

In a saucepan, place the eggs in a single uncrowded layer and add just enough water to cover them. Place over high heat. Just as soon as the water begins to simmer, reduce the heat to maintain a gentle simmer and cook for 15 to 18 minutes. Remove from the heat, drain the eggs, and cover immediately with cold water to halt the cooking. Tap each egg all over to crack the shell, then place under running cold water and peel off the shell.

Each cooked egg makes 1 serving.

Scrambled Eggs

Basic to so many breakfasts, scrambled eggs can be wonderful when properly cooked or rubbery when overcooked. Avoid overcooking, as they will continue to cook after removing from the heat.

Eggs, at room temperature
Milk (not nonfat) or cream
Salt
Unsalted butter
Freshly ground black pepper

Break the eggs into a bowl. For each egg, add 1 teaspoon milk or cream and 1/8 teaspoon salt, or to taste, and beat with a wire whisk or fork until well blended but not frothy.

In a skillet, for each egg, heat 1 teaspoon butter over medium-low heat just until foaming stops. Pour in the eggs. When they begin to set, stir them with a fork, lifting the edges to let uncooked egg pour underneath. Cook the eggs, stirring, just until they are almost set but still creamy. Remove immediately to a heated dish and serve. Pass pepper at the table.

2 scrambled eggs make 1 or 2 servings.

VARIATIONS: Cook onions, shallots, garlic, mushrooms, sweet peppers, ham, or other meat in the butter before adding the eggs. Or add crumbled cooked bacon, grated cheese, toasted sunflower seeds, minced fresh herbs, or slivered truffles when the eggs are almost set. Top plain scrambled eggs with caviar or smoked salmon.

Sweet Pepper and Onion Frittata

Open-faced Italian omelets are cooked over very low heat until set. Serve piping hot or at room temperature.

For the presentation shown here, instead of flipping the *frittata* in the pan, when the top is about half done, make indentions with a spoon and break quail eggs into the indentions. When almost set, finish under the broiler as directed.

¹/₄ cup plus 2 tablespoons olive oil
2 cups thinly sliced onion
1¹/₂ cups julienned red sweet pepper
1 teaspoon minced garlic
¹/₄ cup chopped fresh basil
Salt
8 eggs
3 tablespoons light cream or half and half
¹/₃ cup freshly grated Parmesan cheese, preferably
         Parmigiano-Reggiano
Freshly ground black pepper
2 tablespoons unsalted butter

In a skillet, heat ¹/₄ cup of the olive oil over low heat. Add the onion and sweet pepper and cook until the vegetables are quite tender and slightly caramelized, 35 to 45 minutes. Stir in the garlic, basil, and salt to taste. Remove from the heat and reserve. (This can be done the day before, refrigerated, and reheated in the morning.)

In a bowl, combine the eggs with the cream, cheese, ¹/₂ teaspoon salt, and black pepper to taste and beat until well blended. Set aside.

In a heavy-bottomed 12-inch skillet, preferably nonstick, melt 1 tablespoon of the butter and 1 tablespoon of the remaining oil over medium heat. Distribute the onion and pepper mixture evenly in the bottom of the skillet, then pour the egg mixture over the vegetables. Reduce the heat to low and cook undisturbed until the eggs are set around the edges. Using a spatula, gently lift the edges of the omelet and tilt the pan to let any uncooked egg run down under the bottom. Continue this process until the eggs have almost set on top.

Invert a plate over the top of the pan and then invert the pan and plate together, so the *frittata* is on the plate. Add the remaining 1 tablespoon of butter and oil to the pan and slide the *frittata* back into the pan, cooked side up. Cook until the bottom is set, about 2 minutes. Alternatively, do not turn the *frittata*. Instead place it under a preheated broiler until the top is set, about 30 seconds; be sure to use a flameproof pan and be careful not to burn or overcook the *frittata*.

Loosen the edges of the *frittata* with a spatula and slide it out onto a serving plate. (Or, invert the plate over the pan, invert the pan, and turn the *frittata* out onto the plate.) To serve, cut into wedges.

Makes 4 servings.

Omelets

Once you've mastered the technique, omelets are a quick yet elegant breakfast presentation. If there's a crowd, cook at the table over a portable electric burner. Omelets may be served plain, or with fillings, or topped with a sauce, such as fresh tomato or cheese.

1 tablespoon clarified butter (see note below)
3 eggs
Salt
Freshly ground black or white pepper
Filling (see adjacent suggestions)

In a small bowl, beat the eggs well, then add salt and pepper to taste.

Heat an 8-inch nonstick skillet over high heat. Add the clarified butter and heat until very hot but not smoking. Add the eggs and move the pan continuously over the heat to prevent sticking, using a thin spatula to keep eggs away from the sides of the pan. When the bottom sets up, use the spatula to lift up the sides and let any uncooked egg flow underneath. Just before the top is set, add about 1/3 cup filling down the center of the omelet if you wish. Tilting the pan and using the spatula, roll one third of the omelet over the filling. Hold the pan over the serving plate so the unfolded side begins to slide out. Using the spatula, flip omelet so the folded side folds over with the center on the top; total cooking time should be less than 1 minute. Add a compatible sauce if you wish, and a garnish appropriate to the filling.

Makes 1 omelet, enough for 1 serving.

NOTE: To clarify butter, in a small saucepan, melt 1 cup (2 sticks) butter over low heat. Remove from the heat and let cool for a few minutes, while the milk solids settle to the bottom of the pan. Skim the butterfat from the top and strain the clear (clarified) butter into a container; discard the milk solids. Cover and store in the refrigerator.

FILLINGS FOR OMELETS

Caviar and sour cream.
Steamed or sautéed asparagus tips or broccoli florets.
Grated cheese, one kind or a combination.
Crumbled crisply cooked bacon.
Cooked and shredded chicken, beef, or pork.
Cooked lobster, shrimp, or crab.
Smoked salmon, sour cream, and minced chives.
Minced herbs, one kind or a combination.
Jams or jellies.
Creamed spinach.
Sautéed mushrooms.
Mixed steamed vegetables.
Salsa.
Avocado slices.

Baked or Shirred Eggs

Baking parchment placed over the eggs helps the tops cook evenly.

Eggs
Salt
Freshly ground black pepper or ground cayenne
Unsalted butter, melted
Minced fresh thyme, parsley, or basil, or red sweet pepper
     cut into julienne, for garnish

Preheat an oven to 350° F.

Break each egg into a buttered ramekin or other small baking dish. Season to taste with salt and pepper or cayenne, then cover each egg with 1 teaspoon melted butter. Place the dishes in a baking pan. Transfer to the oven and pour enough hot (not boiling) water into the baking pan to reach about halfway up the sides of the egg dishes. Cover loosely with baking parchment and bake just until the eggs are almost set, about 6 minutes. (The heat from the dish will continue to cook the eggs, so don't overcook in the oven.) Garnish with minced herbs or red pepper strips.

Each cooked egg makes 1 serving.

Eggs with Mild Green Chile Sauce

Here's my variation on the Mexican classic *huevos rancheros*. Prepare the sauce the day before. Accompany with refried beans or chile beans.

GREEN CHILE SAUCE
About 12 fresh tomatillos, or 1 can (13 ounces) tomatillos
2 tablespoons canola or other high-quality vegetable oil
1 cup chopped onion
3 or 4 fresh Anaheim or other mild green chiles,
**   or 1 can (7 ounces) chopped mild green chiles**
1 to 2 teaspoons minced or pressed garlic
1 tablespoon minced fresh oregano, or 1 teaspoon dried
**   oregano leaves (not ground), finely crumbled**
1 tablespoon freshly squeezed lime juice
1/2 teaspoon sugar, or to taste
Salt
1 cup homemade chicken or vegetable stock
**   or canned low-sodium broth**
1 bay leaf

Canola or other high-quality vegetable oil for frying
8 corn tortillas
8 eggs
4 tablespoons (1/2 stick) unsalted butter for frying eggs
3 cups cooked shredded chicken, beef, or pork, warmed (optional)
2 cups freshly shredded Cheddar or Monterey Jack cheese
**   (about 8 ounces), or a combination**
Avocado slices or guacamole (page 80) for garnish
Fresh cilantro (coriander) leaves for garnish

To make the chile sauce, if using fresh tomatillos, remove and discard husks and stems, place in a saucepan, cover with water, and bring to a boil over medium-high heat. Cook until translucent and almost tender, about 5 minutes. Drain, rinse, drain again, and set aside. If using canned tomatillos, drain and set aside.

In a skillet, heat the oil over medium-high heat, add the onion, and cook until soft, about 5 minutes. Transfer to a food processor or blender and add the reserved tomatillos, chiles, garlic, oregano, lime juice, sugar, salt to taste, and 1/2 cup of the stock or broth. Blend until smooth.

Transfer the tomatillo mixture to a saucepan and add the remaining 1/2 cup stock or broth and the bay leaf. Bring to a boil over medium-high heat, then reduce the heat to achieve a simmer, cover, and simmer until slightly thickened and the flavors are well blended, about 30 minutes. Discard the bay leaf. Use the sauce immediately or refrigerate for up to overnight; reheat before using.

Preheat an oven to 200° F.

In a skillet, pour in oil to a depth of 1/2 inch and heat over medium heat. Fry tortillas, one at a time, until crisp and golden. Drain on paper towels and keep warm in the oven.

Fry the eggs in the butter as directed on page 80.

Arrange 2 fried tortillas on each of 4 warmed plates. Add some of the Green Chile Sauce, then top with some of the chicken or other meat (if using). Top each tortilla with a fried egg. Drizzle with more sauce, sprinkle with cheese, and garnish with avocado or guacamole and cilantro. Serve immediately.

Makes 4 servings.

Baked Eggs with Creamed Spinach

Around The Rockpile, we still call this old favorite Eggs Florentine, dating back to the time when just about everything with spinach was termed "Florentine." For a heartier dish, stir about 2 cups chopped cooked chicken or baked ham into the creamed spinach before adding the eggs.

4 pounds fresh spinach, trimmed, or 2 packages (10 ounces *each*)
    frozen chopped spinach
3 ounces cream cheese, at room temperature
Salt
Freshly ground black pepper
4 eggs
2 cups freshly shredded Cheddar cheese (about 6 ounces)

If using fresh spinach, wash thoroughly and place in a pot with whatever washing water clings to the leaves. Cover, and cook over medium-high heat until tender, 3 to 5 minutes. Drain well in a sieve, pressing firmly against the spinach to remove all liquid. Coarsely chop the spinach with a knife. If using thawed frozen spinach, squeeze out as much liquid as possible.

Preheat an oven to 375° F.

In a food processor, combine the spinach and cream cheese and puree until well blended but not too smooth. Add salt and pepper to taste. Distribute the creamed spinach among 4 individual buttered ramekins or other small ovenproof serving dishes. Make a slight indention in the center of each and carefully break 1 egg into each indention. Cover the tops with the cheese. Bake until the eggs are set and the cheese is melted and crusty, about 20 minutes.

Makes 4 servings.

Egyptian Twice-Cooked Eggs

Robie Amer of Chico, California, shared this ultra-rich recipe gleaned from her years in Egypt.

2 tablespoons sesame seeds
3/4 teaspoon ground cumin
1/4 teaspoon freshly grated nutmeg
1/4 teaspoon ground coriander
Salt
Freshly ground black pepper
3/4 cup (11/2 sticks) unsalted butter
12 hard-cooked eggs (page 68), peeled and sliced lengthwise in half
6 small pita breads, warmed and cut horizontally in half

In a small skillet, place the sesame seeds over medium heat and toast, shaking the pan or stirring frequently, until golden, about 5 minutes. Transfer to a plate to cool.

In a small bowl, combine the cumin, nutmeg, coriander, and salt and pepper to taste and set aside.

In a large skillet, melt the butter over low heat. When the butter stops foaming, add the eggs, cut side down, and cook until the eggs begin to brown, 5 to 6 minutes. Turn the eggs and cook, turning and basting occasionally with the butter in the skillet, until browned all over, about 5 minutes longer. While the eggs are cooking, sprinkle them with the spice mixture.

Transfer the eggs to a serving platter, drizzle with the seasoned butter from the skillet, and sprinkle with the toasted sesame seeds. Serve hot with the pita bread.

Makes 6 servings.

Bacon and Eggs Casserole

Here's a new twist on traditional American breakfast fare.

½ cup (1 stick) unsalted butter
8 ounces fresh mushrooms, preferably wild varieties such as
    chanterelles, morels, or shiitakes, sliced
½ pound thick-sliced bacon, preferably pepper-cured, diced
½ cup all-purpose flour
Salt
Freshly ground black pepper
1 quart milk (not nonfat)
12 eggs, lightly beaten
¾ cup light cream or half and half
Fresh chives for garnish

In a sauté pan or skillet, melt 2 tablespoons of the butter over medium-high heat. Add the mushrooms and cook until lightly browned, about 3 minutes. Set aside.

In a skillet, fry the bacon over medium heat until crisp, then drain on paper towels. Discard the bacon fat from the skillet. To the skillet, add 4 tablespoons of the remaining butter, most of the drained bacon (save some for garnishing), and about three quarters of the mushrooms. Mix well and sprinkle with the flour and salt and black pepper to taste. Gradually stir in the milk and cook, stirring constantly, until the mixture is smooth and thickened, about 20 minutes. Cover and set aside.

Preheat an oven to 350° F.

In another skillet, melt the remaining 2 tablespoons butter over medium-low heat. In a bowl, combine the eggs, cream, and 1 teaspoon salt, or to taste. Pour into the skillet and scramble with a fork until barely set; do not overcook. Immediately transfer to a bowl.

In a buttered 9-inch glass soufflé dish, alternately layer the scrambled eggs and the bacon white sauce, ending with sauce. Top with the remaining mushrooms and reserved bacon, then bake, uncovered, until heated through, 15 to 20 minutes. Garnish with chives.

Makes 8 servings.

Scrambled Eggs with Bacon and Vegetables *(Lob Scouse)*

German *lob scouse* is a hearty rendition of bacon and eggs.

½ pound bacon, cut into small pieces
1 cup chopped onion
½ cup chopped green sweet pepper
3 cups diced cooked potatoes, preferably new potatoes
6 to 8 eggs
Salt
Freshly ground black pepper

In a large skillet, cook the bacon over medium heat until crisp, then add the onion and sweet pepper and cook until the vegetables are soft, about 5 minutes. Add the cooked potatoes and continue cooking until heated through.

Break the eggs into a bowl and beat lightly. Pour into the bacon mixture and scramble with a fork until just set. Season to taste with salt and pepper. Serve immediately.

Makes 6 servings.

Poached Eggs

Poached eggs are delicious on their own and even better when smothered in Hollandaise sauce as directed in the adjacent recipes.

1 tablespoon white wine vinegar
Eggs, at room temperature

In a large skillet or sauté pan, pour in water to a depth of about $2\frac{1}{2}$ inches. Add the vinegar and bring to a boil over medium-high heat, then reduce the heat so that the water barely bubbles. Break an egg into a small bowl. Using the tip of a slotted spoon, swirl a section of the water to activate it, then immediately slip the egg into the center of the whirlpool. Repeat with as many eggs as desired without crowding the pan. Reduce the heat to low and let the eggs steep in the hot water until the whites are set, about 3 minutes. Remove the eggs from the water with a slotted spoon. Drain well and serve at once.

Each cooked egg makes 1 serving.

Hollandaise Sauce

For a change of pace, this velvety sauce can be made with orange juice.

4 egg yolks
3 tablespoons freshly squeezed lemon juice
1 cup (2 sticks) cold unsalted butter, cut into 8 equal pieces
Ground cayenne

Pour 2 inches of water into the bottom part of a double boiler and bring to a simmer over medium-high heat, then adjust the heat to maintain a simmer.

In the top part of the double boiler, combine the egg yolks, lemon juice, and 2 pieces of the butter. Place over the simmering water and stir rapidly with a wire whisk until the butter melts. Add the remaining pieces of butter, one at a time, stirring until each melts

before adding the next piece. When all the butter has been added, stir in a pinch of cayenne. Keep warm over warm water until ready to serve. If the sauce gets too thick or begins to curdle before serving, briskly stir in a small amount of boiling water until smooth.

Makes about 2 cups of sauce, enough for 8 servings.

Hollandaise Classics

Prepare Hollandaise Sauce and poach eggs as directed in the adjacent recipes, then combine them with a variety of other ingredients as suggested here to create some of America's favorite fancy breakfast dishes. Whichever combination you choose, be sure to serve immediately after assembling.

EGGS BENEDICT: Toast and butter rounds of Holland rusk or English muffin halves. Cover each round with a slice of broiled ham or Canadian bacon. Top with a poached egg, then cover with Hollandaise Sauce.

EGGS BLACKSTONE: Toast and butter English muffin halves. Top each with a slice of broiled tomato, then crumbled crisply fried bacon, and a poached egg. Cover with Hollandaise Sauce and garnish with a bit of crumbled bacon.

EGGS SARDOU: Place 1 or 2 cooked large artichoke bottoms on each plate. Top each bottom with a little warm creamed spinach, then a poached egg. Cover with Hollandaise Sauce.

EGGS WITH SALMON: Fill freshly baked puff pastry shells with slivered smoked salmon, top with a poached egg, and cover with Hollandaise Sauce. Garnish with additional salmon and fresh caviar.

EGGS ON SCONES: Split warm Scones (page 31), top with slices of fried Country Ham (page 83), and then place a poached egg on each. Cover with Hollandaise Sauce made with orange juice and garnish with thin strips of orange zest.

EGGS ST. CHARLES: Panfry small rainbow trout (page 91), top each with 1 or 2 poached eggs, and cover with Hollandaise Sauce.

Scrambled Eggs on Guacamole Toast

Here's a colorful presentation of scrambled eggs.

GUACAMOLE
1 ripe avocado
$1/2$ cup peeled, seeded, drained, and chopped ripe tomato
2 tablespoons minced red onion
2 tablespoons freshly squeezed lime juice, or to taste
Salt
Ground cayenne or other hot chile

6 eggs
$1/4$ cup milk or cream
Freshly ground black pepper
2 tablespoons unsalted butter
$1/4$ cup chopped red onion
4 slices firm-textured, whole-grain bread
4 slices ripe tomato
Fresh cilantro (coriander) sprigs for garnish

To make the Guacamole, scoop the avocado pulp into a bowl. Using a fork, mash the avocado coarsely, leaving a few small chunky pieces. Gently stir in the chopped tomato, minced onion, lime juice, and salt and chile to taste. Set aside.

In another bowl, combine the eggs, milk or cream, and salt and black pepper to taste and beat well. Set aside.

In a skillet, melt the butter over medium-high heat. Add the chopped onion and sauté until soft but not browned, about 5 minutes. Reduce the heat to medium, pour in the egg mixture, and scramble with a fork until just set. Immediately transfer to a bowl.

Meanwhile, toast the bread and keep warm.

To serve, spread about 1 tablespoon of the Guacamole over each slice of toast. Top each with a portion of the scrambled eggs, a slice of tomato, and a dollop of Guacamole. Garnish with cilantro.

Makes 4 servings.

Fried Eggs

Whether you enjoy them sunny-side up with soft runny yolks or flipped over and cooked until the yolk is set, frying over fairly low heat will keep the whites tender. You may use a larger skillet to cook more eggs at a time; just be sure to add enough butter and give each egg plenty of space in the pan.

Eggs
Unsalted butter

Place an 8-inch, preferably nonstick, skillet over medium-low heat. When the pan is hot, add 1 tablespoon butter. When the butter stops foaming, carefully crack 1 or 2 eggs into the pan. As soon as the whites begin to set, shake the pan or move the eggs with a spatula to prevent sticking. Cook, basting with butter if desired, until the yolks are set to preference, 3 to 4 minutes for sunny-side up. Or cook until the yolks are almost set, then turn and cook several seconds for over-easy eggs or up to 1 minute for over-hard eggs.

2 fried eggs make 1 or 2 servings.

MEAT, FISH & POULTRY

Country Ham

American country-cured hams are quite strongly flavored, a far cry from the water-injected, overnight-cured hams of the supermarket. Fresh hams are seasoned with salt and pepper, then hung to slowly dry in the fragrant smoke of hickory, oak, apple, and other woods. Next, they're aged for a year or more. As they dry and shrink, they achieve the intense flavor that has rivaled prosciutto and other fine European specialty hams in quality, taste, and reputation for three hundred years. In times when demand was less intense, hams often aged or cured for as long as seven years, ending up coated with black mold.

Aged hams must be soaked, then thoroughly scrubbed and rinsed off before being boiled or steamed. Next the skin is removed and the hams are baked, with or without a glaze, or sliced and panfried.

A 10- to 12-pound country-cured ham, aged 4 to 12 months

In a deep container, combine the ham with enough cold water to cover, and soak: overnight for hams that have aged less than 6 months; 2 to 3 days for hams that have aged from 6 to 12 months. Discard the soaking water.

Preheat an oven to 500° F.

With a stiff brush under cold running water, vigorously scrub the ham to remove any dust or mold as well as the pepper coating. Place in a large roasting pan, add about 6 cups water, cover tightly with a lid or aluminum foil, and place in the preheated oven for 20 minutes. Then turn off the heat, leaving the ham in the closed oven for about 3 hours.

Turn the oven on again to 500° F for 15 minutes, then turn off the heat, leaving the ham in the oven for another 3 hours or up to overnight.

Remove the ham from the pan and trim off the rind with a sharp knife. Slice and eat as is, or store in the refrigerator and slice and fry whenever you wish.

Alternatively, cover the baked and trimmed ham with a favorite glaze and bake in a 375° F oven, basting occasionally with the drippings, until the glaze is set and browned, about 20 minutes.

Makes about 20 servings.

Fried Country Ham with Red-Eye Gravy

Thin gravy made from the frying drippings is dubbed "red eye" after the pool that forms in the center of the skillet. Sometimes a bit of coffee is added to flavor and darken the gravy. Serve the gravy over the ham and grits or hot biscuits.

4 country ham slices, 1/4-inch thick (see adjacent recipe)
1 or 2 tablespoons black coffee (optional)

In a heavy skillet, place the ham slices over low heat and cook until tender and lightly browned, about 20 minutes. Remove the ham to a plate and keep warm.

To make the gravy, add about 1 cup water and the coffee (if using) to the skillet. Increase the heat to medium-high and bring to a boil, stirring to loosen all the browned bits. Cook about 2 minutes. Serve warm.

Makes 4 servings.

Scrapple

Originally, leftover parts of pork, including necks, shoulders, and feet, went into this Pennsylvania Dutch breakfast dish. This simple version that relies on good pork sausage was shared by Barbara Fritz and was a special favorite of her father, Emanuel. Since helping to decorate for his hundredth birthday celebration, I've wondered if eating scrapple for breakfast contributes to longevity in spite of the high cholesterol content.

1 pound bulk pork sausage, mild or hot
1 1/2 cups yellow cornmeal
1 tablespoon minced fresh sage, or 1 teaspoon crumbled dried sage
1 tablespoon minced fresh marjoram, or 1 teaspoon crumbled dried marjoram
1 1/2 teaspoons minced fresh thyme, or 1/2 teaspoon crumbled dried thyme
Salt
Freshly ground black pepper
About 1/2 cup (1 stick) butter for frying
Pure maple syrup, warmed (optional)

Break up the sausage and transfer to a large stockpot. Add 5 cups water, place over high heat, and bring to a boil, then adjust the heat to maintain a simmer. While stirring continuously with a long-handled wooden spoon, add the cornmeal in a slow, steady stream. Add the sage, marjoram, thyme, and salt and pepper to taste. Simmer, stirring frequently, until thickened, about 15 minutes. Cover and simmer, stirring frequently, until very thick, about 1 hour.

Pour the mixture into a lightly greased 9-by-5-inch loaf pan, pressing it evenly into the corners. Cover with plastic wrap and refrigerate overnight or for up to 3 days.

To remove the scrapple loaf, briefly dip the pan into hot water and slide a blunt knife around the edges. Invert the scrapple onto a flat surface and remove the pan. Slice the loaf as you would bread.

Preheat an oven to 200° F.

In a large skillet over medium-high heat, melt the butter, about 2 tablespoons at a time as needed. When the butter stops foaming, add a few scrapple slices at a time and fry until golden brown on one side, 8 to 10 minutes. Turn and brown the other sides, 8 to 10 minutes longer. Transfer to an ovenproof dish and keep warm in the oven until all the slices are cooked, adding the remaining butter as needed. Serve warm, with warmed maple syrup (if using).

Makes 6 to 8 servings.

Panfried Pork Tenderloin

For a change of pace from bacon, ham, or sausage, serve this fresh pork dish with warmed chunky applesauce, or apple slices sautéed with onion.

1 pork tenderloin, sliced 1/2-inch thick
Salt
Freshly ground black pepper
Flour for dredging
1/4 cup (1/2 stick) unsalted butter

Season the pork slices with salt and pepper to taste, then dredge in flour. Heat the butter in a skillet over medium-high heat, add the pork slices, and cook, turning occasionally, until tender and just past the pink stage inside, about 5 minutes.

Makes 4 to 6 servings.

Apple-Pork Sausage Patties

Store the mixture in the refrigerator, breaking off as much as needed at any one time; use within a week.

1½ pounds ground pork butt, with some fat
¼ cup unsweetened frozen apple juice concentrate, thawed
½ teaspoon salt, or to taste
½ teaspoon freshly ground black pepper, or to taste
⅛ teaspoon ground cayenne, or to taste
1 tablespoon minced fresh sage, or 1 teaspoon crumbled dried sage
1½ teaspoons minced fresh thyme, or ½ teaspoon crumbled dried thyme
¼ teaspoon ground allspice

In a large bowl, combine the ground pork, apple juice, salt, pepper, cayenne, sage, thyme, and allspice. Mix well, using your hands if necessary to blend the spices into the meat. Break off a bit of the mixture and cook in a hot skillet, then taste. Adjust seasonings to taste. Wrap well and refrigerate for several hours or overnight to blend the flavors.

Break off pieces of the sausage, roll into 1½-inch balls, and flatten.

To cook, add just enough water to barely cover the bottom of a heavy skillet. Add several sausage patties and cook over medium-high heat until the water evaporates. Reduce the heat to low and cook, turning, until the patties are brown and crusty. Transfer to a wire rack set on a baking sheet to drain well and blot with paper toweling to remove excess surface fat.

Makes about 24 patties.

Fried Bacon

Whenever possible, have high-quality bacon freshly sliced from a slab at a good meat market. Initial high heat quickly renders as much fat as possible, then slow cooking in a pan kept free of excess rendering fat yields the tastiest and crispiest bacon.

½ pound bacon, preferably thick-sliced

Heat a heavy skillet over high heat. Arrange the bacon slices in a single layer and cook for 1 to 2 minutes. Reduce the heat to medium-low and cook, turning several times and draining off excess fat as it is rendered, until the bacon is crisp or done to preference. Transfer to a wire rack set on a baking sheet to drain well and blot with paper toweling to remove excess surface fat.

Makes 4 servings.

ALTERNATIVES: Arrange the bacon slices in a single layer on a rack in a baking pan and cook in a 400° F oven until crisp, about 10 minutes, or place under a preheated broiler and cook, turning once, until crisp, about 4 minutes.

To cook in a microwave oven, arrange the slices in a single layer on 4 sheets of paper toweling and loosely cover with a single sheet of paper toweling. Cook at 100 percent power for times suggested by the oven manufacturer, 2 to 6 minutes, according to type of oven.

Fried Coppa

Coppa is an Italian-style pork product that's usually thinly sliced and eaten cold. Fried, it's a flavorful change of pace from bacon and a particular favorite of literary agent Martha Casselman.

½ pound thinly sliced coppa

Heat a heavy skillet over medium-high heat, add the coppa, and cook, turning frequently, until the meat is crinkly, about 4 minutes. Transfer to a wire rack set on a baking sheet to drain well.

Makes 4 servings.

Corned Beef Hash

I prefer hash without the traditional crust from overcooking. If you feel differently, cook on one side until brown and crusty, invert, and cook the other side until crusty. Hash is one dish that I enjoy with tomato catsup.

1 pound unpeeled red potatoes
2 tablespoons canola or other high-quality vegetable oil
1/4 cup (1/2 stick) unsalted butter
1 cup sliced onion
2 medium red sweet peppers, cut into julienne
1 teaspoon minced garlic
3 to 4 cups cooked corned beef brisket, thinly sliced, then cut into
    julienne
1 tablespoon minced fresh thyme, or 1 teaspoon crumbled dried
    thyme
Salt
Freshly ground black pepper or ground cayenne
1 tablespoon Worcestershire sauce, or to taste
1/2 cup chopped fresh flat-leaf parsley
4 to 6 poached eggs (page 78)
Fresh parsley or thyme sprigs for garnish

In a saucepan, boil the potatoes in water to cover until they are tender but still hold together, about 15 minutes. Drain and let cool, then slice and cut into julienne.

In a sauté pan or skillet, heat the oil and 2 tablespoons of the butter over medium heat. Add the onion and sweet peppers and cook, stirring occasionally, until the vegetables are very soft but not browned, about 10 minutes. Stir in the garlic and cook 1 minute. Add the remaining 2 tablespoons butter, the reserved potatoes, corned beef, thyme, and salt, pepper or cayenne, and Worcestershire sauce to taste. Cook until the meat and potatoes are heated through, about 8 minutes. Stir in the chopped parsley and distribute among 4 to 6 individual plates. Top with a poached egg and garnish with parsley or thyme sprigs.

Makes 4 to 6 servings.

VARIATION: Substitute shredded cooked chicken for the corned beef.

Joe's Special

Serve this old San Francisco favorite with warmed crusty sourdough bread and good sweet butter.

2 tablespoons olive oil
1 1/2 cups chopped onion
1 1/2 pounds ground beef, crumbled
1 teaspoon minced garlic
1/2 pound mushrooms, sliced
2 pounds coarsely chopped spinach, cooked, or 1 package
    (10 ounces) frozen spinach, thawed
1 1/2 teaspoons minced fresh oregano, or 1/2 teaspoon crumbled
    dried oregano
Salt
Freshly ground black pepper
Freshly grated nutmeg
5 eggs, lightly beaten
Freshly grated Parmesan cheese for passing

In a sauté pan or skillet, heat the oil over medium-high heat. Add the onion and cook until soft but not browned, about 5 minutes. Add the ground beef, garlic, and mushrooms, and sauté until the meat is lightly browned, just past the pink stage, about 5 minutes. Squeeze the spinach to remove excess liquid, then add it to the pan and cook, stirring, for 3 minutes. Add the oregano, and salt, pepper, and nutmeg to taste. Reduce the heat to low and add the eggs, stirring until the eggs are just set but still soft. Serve immediately. Pass the cheese at the table for sprinkling over the top.

Makes 6 servings.

Grillades and Grits

Old Creole New Orleans gave America this special breakfast dish of braised veal, which is always accompanied by grits to soak up the rich gravy. Lard is still used for sautéing the veal in many New Orleans kitchens in place of the oil and butter.

6 boneless veal round steaks (5 to 6 ounces *each*),
about 1/2-inch thick
Salt
Freshly ground black pepper
Ground cayenne
Flour for dredging
3 tablespoons canola or other high-quality vegetable oil
3 tablespoons unsalted butter
2 1/2 cups chopped onion
1 1/2 tablespoons minced garlic
2 cups peeled, seeded, drained, and chopped ripe or canned tomato
2 cups homemade veal or chicken stock or canned reduced-sodium
chicken broth
1 bay leaf
1 1/2 cups grits, cooked according to package directions

Trim away all fat from the veal and cut the meat into pieces 2 to 3 inches in diameter. Place the meat between 2 sheets of waxed paper and pound with a mallet or other flat instrument to a thickness of about 1/8 inch. Generously season with salt, pepper, and cayenne. Dip the meat into the flour to coat lightly, shaking off excess flour.

In a sauté pan or skillet, heat 1 tablespoon of the oil and 1 tablespoon of the butter over medium heat. Add the veal pieces a few at a time and brown on both sides. Transfer to a platter as they are browned; reserve.

Add the remaining oil and butter to the pan and heat over medium-high heat. Add the onion and cook until soft but not browned, about 5 minutes. Stir in the garlic and cook 1 minute. Add the tomato, stock or broth, and bay leaf, and bring the mixture to a boil, then partially cover, reduce the heat to maintain a simmer, and simmer for 20 minutes.

Add the reserved veal and simmer, partially covered, turning the veal every 10 minutes to coat with the gravy, until the flavors are well blended and the meat is tender when pierced with a sharp knife, about 30 minutes. Remove the meat to a heated platter and keep warm.

Reheat the gravy just before serving. Mound the cooked grits on heated individual plates, add the veal grillades, cover both with the gravy, and serve immediately.

Makes 6 servings.

Breakfast Steaks

Serve with your favorite potatoes and baked (page 70), fried (page 80), or poached (page 78) eggs.

Salt
Freshly ground black pepper
4 slices beef fillet, about 3 ounces *each*
1/4 cup Worcestershire sauce
2 tablespoons unsalted butter
Juice of 1 lemon

Place a skillet over high heat until very hot. Salt and pepper the fillets on both sides to taste, pressing the seasoning in with your fingers. Place the steaks in the hot pan and immediately reduce the heat to low. Sear briefly on one side, about 45 seconds, turn the steaks, and sear the other sides. Continue cooking, turning occasionally, until the steaks are done to your taste, about 5 minutes total cooking time for medium-rare. While the steaks are cooking, sprinkle with the Worcestershire sauce, top each with butter, and add the lemon juice. Serve the steaks immediately, drizzling with any pan juices that are left.

Makes 4 servings.

Smoked Fish with Rice *(Kedgeree)*

Anglo-Indian in origin, *kedgeree* is traditionally made with finnan haddie (smoked haddock). I dislike the strong smell and flavor of finnan haddie, and prefer the dish made with smoked trout, sablefish, or whitefish. Offer your favorite fruit chutney at the table.

1/2 pound smoked fish, flaked
2 cups cooked long-grain brown or white rice
4 ounces smoked ham, cut into julienne
1/2 cup chopped fresh flat-leaf parsley
1/4 cup (1/2 stick) unsalted butter, melted
1/4 cup heavy (whipping) cream, light cream, or half and half
Salt
Ground cayenne
3 hard-cooked eggs (page 68), sliced or grated
Fresh flat-leaf parsley sprigs for garnish

Preheat an oven to 350° F. Butter a 2-quart baking dish and set aside.

In a large bowl, combine the flaked fish, rice, ham, chopped parsley, butter, cream, and salt and cayenne to taste. Toss thoroughly to combine, then transfer to the prepared dish. Arrange the eggs on top, cover tightly with a lid or aluminum foil, and bake until hot, about 20 minutes. Garnish with parsley sprigs before serving.

Makes 4 to 6 servings.

Panfried Fish

Although trout is the most popular breakfast fish, almost any fish makes a tasty addition to the breakfast table. In addition to this method, try grilling, steaming, or poaching your favorite fish. Be sure the fish is very fresh, and avoid overcooking; fish is done when the flesh just turns opaque.

4 fresh rainbow trout or other small whole fish (10- to 12-ounces
    ***each*) with heads and tails intact, dressed and boned**
Salt
Freshly ground black pepper
Flour for dredging
Peanut or other high-quality vegetable oil for frying
Unsalted butter for frying
1/2 cup (1 stick) unsalted butter
3 tablespoons freshly squeezed lemon juice
1/4 cup minced fresh flat-leaf parsley
Thinly sliced lemon for garnish
Fresh flat-leaf parsley sprigs for garnish

Quickly rinse the fish under cold running water and pat dry with paper toweling. Sprinkle with salt and pepper and lightly dredge with flour.

In a skillet large enough to hold the fish, combine equal parts oil and butter to a depth of 1/4 inch and place over medium-high heat. When the butter stops foaming, add the fish, and cook, turning once, until golden brown on both sides. Remove the fish to heated plates.

Quickly discard the cooking fat and wipe out the skillet with paper toweling. Place over medium-high heat, add the 1/2 cup butter, and cook, scraping up any browned bits from the pan, until the butter is very lightly browned. Stir in the lemon juice and minced parsley and pour over the trout. Garnish with lemon slices and parsley sprigs and serve immediately.

Makes 4 servings.

Braised Quail

For as long as I can remember, my mother has cooked quail like this for Christmas breakfast.

4 strips thick-sliced bacon
8 quail, ready to cook
Salt
Freshly ground black pepper
Flour for dredging
¼ cup (½ stick) unsalted butter
½ pound fresh mushrooms, preferably wild types such as chanterelles, morels, or shiitakes, sliced
1 cup homemade chicken stock or canned reduced-sodium broth
1 tablespoon minced fresh thyme, or 1 teaspoon crumbled dried thyme
½ cup heavy (whipping) cream, light cream, or half and half
8 pieces Fried Polenta (page 56) or toasted whole wheat bread (optional)
Fresh thyme or flat-leaf parsley sprigs for garnish

In a skillet, fry the bacon as directed on page 85 until crisp, then crumble and set aside.

Sprinkle the quail with salt and pepper, then lightly dredge with flour.

In a heavy pot with a tight-fitting cover, heat the butter over medium-high heat. Add the birds and brown on all sides, about 5 minutes. Transfer the quail to a plate and set aside. Add the mushrooms to the pot and cook until tender, about 5 minutes. Add the stock or broth, thyme, and cream and stir to blend well. Return the quail to the pot, cover, and cook over low heat, turning the quail frequently, until the meat is tender when pierced with a fork, 45 minutes to 1 hour. Transfer the quail to a warm platter. Increase the heat to medium-high and stir until the sauce is slightly reduced.

To serve, place the quail on fried polenta or toast (if using) and spoon the sauce over the top. Sprinkle with the crumbled bacon and garnish with thyme or parsley sprigs.

Makes 4 to 8 servings.

Brabant Potatoes

This garlicky dish from New Orleans is a hearty accompaniment to meat or egg dishes, and a good change from ubiquitous hash browns.

¼ cup (½ stick) unsalted butter
1 teaspoon minced garlic
4 medium-sized white potatoes
Peanut or other high-quality vegetable oil for frying
2 tablespoons minced fresh flat-leaf parsley
Salt
Ground cayenne

In a small sauté pan or skillet, melt the butter over low heat. Add the garlic and cook for about 5 minutes; do not allow the garlic to brown. Strain; reserve the butter and discard the garlic.

Peel the potatoes and cut into 1-inch cubes. Place in iced water to crisp, then pat dry with paper toweling.

In a deep fryer or skillet, pour in oil to a depth of 2 inches and heat to 320° F.

Add the potatoes to the hot oil and fry until soft and pale yellow, about 3 minutes. Using a slotted utensil, transfer to paper toweling to drain well.

Increase the temperature of the oil to 375° F. and preheat an oven to 200° F.

Add the drained potatoes to the oil and fry until crisp and golden, about 3 minutes. Using a slotted utensil, transfer to fresh paper toweling to drain again.

In a deep bowl, toss the well-drained potatoes with the reserved garlic butter, the parsley, and salt and cayenne to taste. Transfer to a baking sheet lined with paper toweling and place in the oven for the flavors to blend for about 20 minutes before serving.

Makes 6 servings.

RECIPE INDEX

Ham, Country 83
Ham, Fried Country 83
Hard-Cooked Eggs 68
Hash, Corned Beef 87
Herbal Tea 10
Hollandaise Sauce 78
Hot Chocolate, French 11
Hot Cocoa, Mexican 11
Hot Mulled Cider 10
Hot Multi-Grain Cereal 23

Indian Pudding 52

Jam, Fruit 20
Joe's Special 87
Johnnycakes 40

Kedgeree 91
Koschaf 19

Lemon or Lime Curd 20
Lemon Sauce 55
Lemon Soufflé Pancakes 37
Lob Scouse 77

Mexican Hot Cocoa 11
Mimosa 13
Monkey Bread 44
Morning Sorbets 17
Muffins, Berry 24
Muffins, Bran 24
Muffins, Fresh Apple 26
Muffins, Orange-Glazed Prune 26
Muffins, Spicy Cocoa 27

New Orleans Raised Rice Cakes *(Calas)* 58

Oatmeal, Fruity 23
Oatmeal Loaf 28
Omelets 70
Orange Butter 31
Orange-Glazed Prune Muffins 26

Pancakes, Blueberry Corn 40
Pancakes, Buttermilk 37
Pancakes, Four-Grain 39
Pancakes, Lemon Soufflé 37
Pancakes, Puffed Oven-Baked 41
Pancakes, Round Danish *(Aebleskiver)* 39
Panfried Fish 91
Panfried Pork Tenderloin 84
Poached Eggs 78
Polenta, Fried 56
Popovers 27
Pork Tenderloin, Panfried 84
Potatoes, Brabant 92
Preserves, Fig 20
Pudding, Breakfast Bread 55
Pudding, Creamy Rice 52
Pudding, Indian 52
Puffed Oven-Baked Pancakes 41

Quail, Braised 92

Ramos Fizz 14
Red-Eye Gravy 83
Rice Cakes, New Orleans Raised 58
Rice, Smoked Fish with 91
Rice Pudding Brulée, Creamy 52
Ricotta Cheese Torta 67
Round Danish Pancakes *(Aebleskiver)* 39

Sauce, Lemon 55
Sauce, Warm Berry 55
Sausage Patties, Apple-Pork 85

Scones with Orange Butter 31
Scrambled Eggs 68
Scrambled Eggs on Guacamole Toast 80
Scrambled Eggs with Bacon and Vegetables
    (Lob Scouse) 77
Scrapple 84
Shirred Eggs, Baked or 70
Skillet Cake with Sautéed Apples 42
Smoked Fish with Rice *(Kedgeree)* 91
Smoothy, Yogurt 14
Soft-Cooked Eggs 68
Sorbets, Morning 17
Soufflé, Cheese 64
Sour Cream Breakfast Cake with Pecan and
    Cinnamon Filling 49
Sparkling Citrus Blend 13
Spicy Cocoa Muffins 27
Steaks, Breakfast 88
Sticky Buns 46
Sweet Pepper and Onion Frittata 69
Swiss Cold Oat Cereal 22

Tea 10
Toast, French 56
Toast Toppings 44
Torta, Ricotta Cheese 67

Upside-Down Breakfast Cake 51

Waffles, Butter-Rich 36
Warm Berry Sauce 55
Whole Wheat Zucchini Bread 28

Yeast Biscuits 30
Yogurt Smoothy 14

Zucchini Bread, Whole Wheat 28

ACKNOWLEDGMENTS

To Bill LeBlond, my longtime editor, and the rest of my friends at Chronicle Books for giving me the opportunity to revise this book.

To Martha Casselman, my literary agent on the original edition, for initiating the project with Arbor House/Morrow and loaning her great dishes and other props.

To Kathie Ness for superb and speedy copyediting of the original edition.

To Patricia Brabant and her assistant Louis Block for a gorgeous collaboration and for making each photo session seem more like a party than a workday.

To Gail High, kitchen assistant, for managing to keep the studio kitchen functioning during the photography and for finally noticing the skillet of *frittata* that had been hanging on the pot rack for days.

To Cleve Gallat for his keen sense of design details in creating the typography for both editions.

To those who shared recipes, sampled recipe testing, gave numerous suggestions, and offered encouragement throughout the original and revised editions, especially Robie Amer, Ed Broussard, Don Bull, Joyce and Berke Carr, John Carr, Barbara Fritz, Naila Gallagher, Louis Hicks, Christine and Ken High, Gail and Tad High, Jim Hildreth, Douglas Jackson, Doris Keith, Mark Leno, Marilyn Babs Lonon, Mary Val McCoy, James and Lucille McNair, Martha and Devereux McNair, Stephen Marcus, Marian May, Lenny Meyer, Jack Porter, Tom and Nancy Reiss, John and Ryan Richardson, Bob and Kristi Spence, Burt Tessler, Jim Wentworth, and Kathryn Wittenmyer.

And to my crew at The Rockpile Press, both past and present—Lin Cotton, Addie Prey, Buster Booroo, Dweasel Pickle, Joshua J. Chew, Michael T. Wigglebutt, Beauregard Ezekiel Valentine, Miss Olivia de Puss Puss, Miss Vivien "Bunny" Fleigh, and Andrew Moore—for all their loyal services throughout recipe development and testing, writing, editing, photographing, and revising.

The linens, bed tray, and tableware on the back cover, as well as the flatware and napkin on the cover and several pieces throughout the book, were graciously provided by Fillamento, San Francisco.

Many vintage kitchen pieces in the book are from the collection of Dishes Delmar and owners Burt Tessler and Jim Wentworth.

Other props are from the private collections of Martha Casselman, Glen Carrol and Patricia Brabant, Christine High, and Gail and Tad High.